*

A CHILD'S GARDEN
OF VERSES

*

The SAMOA EDITION of the WORKS of
Robert Louis Stevenson

A Child's
Garden of Verses

AND

Short Stories

INTERNATIONAL READERS LEAGUE

NEW YORK

THE SAMOA EDITION

1947

Printed in the United States of America

CONTENTS

A CHILD'S GARDEN OF VERSES

I

BED IN SUMMER

IN winter I get up at night
And dress by yellow candle-light.
In summer, quite the other way,
I have to go to bed by day.

I have to go to bed and see
The birds still hopping on the tree,
Or hear the grown-up people's feet
Still going past me in the street.

And does it not seem hard to you,
When all the sky is clear and blue,
And I should like so much to play,
To have to go to bed by day?

II

A THOUGHT

IT is very nice to think
The world is full of meat and drink,
With little children saying grace
In every Christian kind of place.

III

AT THE SEASIDE

WHEN I was down beside the sea
A wooden spade they gave to me
　To dig the sandy shore.
My holes were empty like a cup,
In every hole the sea came up,
　Till it could come no more.

IV

YOUNG NIGHT THOUGHT

ALL night long and every night,
When my mamma puts out the light,
I see the people marching by,
As plain as day, before my eye.

Armies and emperors and kings,
All carrying different kinds of things,
And marching in so grand a way,
You never saw the like by day.

So fine a show was never seen,
At the great circus on the green;
For every kind of beast and man
Is marching in that caravan.

At first they move a little slow,
But still the faster on they go,
And still beside them close I keep
Until we reach the town of Sleep.

V

WHOLE DUTY OF CHILDREN

A CHILD should always say what's true
And speak when he is spoken to,
And behave mannerly at table:
At least as far as he is able.

VI

RAIN

THE rain is raining all around,
  It falls on field and tree,
It rains on the umbrellas here,
  And on the ships at sea.

VII

PIRATE STORY

THREE of us afloat in the meadow by the swing,
  Three of us aboard in the basket on the lea,
Winds are in the air, they are blowing in the spring,
  And waves are on the meadow like the waves there
    are at sea.

Where shall we adventure, to-day that we're afloat,
  Wary of the weather and steering by a star?
Shall it be to Africa, a-steering of the boat,
  To Providence, or Babylon, or off to Malabar?

Hi! but here's a squadron a-rowing on the sea—
  Cattle on the meadow a-charging with a roar!
Quick, and we'll escape them, they're as mad as they
      can be,
The wicket is the harbor and the garden is the shore.

VIII

FOREIGN LANDS

UP into the cherry tree
Who should climb but little me?
I held the trunk with both my hands
And looked abroad on foreign lands.

I saw the next door garden lie,
Adorned with flowers before my eye,
And many pleasant places more
That I had never seen before.

I saw the dimpling river pass
And be the sky's blue looking-glass;
The dusty roads go up and down
With people tramping into town.

If I could find a higher tree
Further and further I should see,

To where the grown up river slips
Into the sea among the ships,

To where the roads on either hand
Lead onward into fairy land,
Where all the children dine at five,
And all the playthings come alive.

IX

WINDY NIGHTS

WHENEVER the moon and stars are set,
  Whenever the wind is high,
All night long in the dark and wet,
  A man goes riding by.
Late in the night when the fires are out,
Why does he gallop and gallop about?

Whenever the trees are crying aloud,
  And ships are tossed at sea,
By, on the highway, low and loud,
  By at the gallop goes he.
By at the gallop he goes, and then
By he comes back at the gallop again.

X

TRAVEL

I SHOULD like to rise and go
Where the golden apples grow;—

Where below another sky
Parrot islands anchored lie,
And, watched by cockatoos and goats,
Lonely Crusoes building boats;—
Where in sunshine reaching out
Eastern cities, miles about,
Are with mosque and minaret
Among sandy gardens set,
And the rich goods from near and far
Hang for sale in the bazaar;—
Where the Great Wall round China goes,
And on one side the desert blows,
And with bell and voice and drum,
Cities on the other hum;—
Where are forests, hot as fire,
Wide as England, tall as a spire,
Full of apes and cocoa-nuts
And the negro hunters' huts;—
Where the knotty crocodile
Lies and blinks in the Nile,
And the red flamingo flies
Hunting fish before his eyes;—
Where in jungles, near and far,
Man-devouring tigers are,
Lying close and giving ear
Lest the hunt be drawing near,
Or a comer-by be seen
Swinging in a palanquin;—
Where among the desert sands
Some deserted city stands,

All its children, sweep and prince
Grown to manhood ages since,
Not a foot in street or house,
Not a stir of child or mouse,
And when kindly falls the night,
In all the town no spark of light.
There I'll come when I'm a man
With a camel caravan;
Light a fire in the gloom
Of some dusty dining-room;
See the pictures on the walls,
Heroes, fights and festivals;
And in a corner find the toys
Of the old Egyptian boys.

XI

SINGING

OF speckled eggs the birdie sings
    And nests among the trees;
The sailor sings of ropes and things
    In ships upon the seas.

The children sing in far Japan,
    The children sing in Spain;
The organ with the organ man
    Is singing in the rain.

XII

LOOKING FORWARD

WHEN I am grown to man's estate
I shall be very proud and great,
And tell the other girls and boys
Not to meddle with my toys.

XIII

A GOOD PLAY

WE built a ship upon the stairs
All made of the back-bedroom chairs,
And filled it full of sofa pillows
To go a-sailing on the billows.

We took a saw and several nails,
And water in the nursery pails;
And Tom said, "Let us also take
An apple and a slice of cake;"—
Which was enough for Tom and me
To go a-sailing on, till tea.

We sailed along for days and days
And had the very best of plays;
But Tom fell out and hurt his knee,
So there was no one left but me.

XIV

WHERE GO THE BOATS?

DARK brown is the river,
　Golden is the sand.
It flows along forever,
　With trees on either hand.

Green leaves a-floating,
　Castles of the foam,
Boats of mine a-boating—
　Where will all come home?

On goes the river
　And out past the mill,
Away down the valley,
　Away down the hill.

Away down the river,
　A hundred miles or more,
Other little children
　Shall bring my boats ashore.

XV

AUNTIE'S SKIRTS

WHENEVER Auntie moves around,
Her dresses make a curious sound;
They trail behind her up the floor,
And trundle after through the door.

XVI

THE LAND OF COUNTERPANE

WHEN I was sick and lay a-bed,
I had two pillows at my head,
And all my toys beside me lay
To keep me happy all the day.

And sometimes for an hour or so
I watched my leaden soldiers go,
With different uniforms and drills,
Among the bed-clothes through the hills;

And sometimes sent my ships in fleets
All up and down among the sheets;
Or brought my trees and houses out,
And planted cities all about.

I was the giant great and still
That sits upon the pillow-hill,
And sees before him, dale and plain,
The pleasant land of counterpane.

XVII

THE LAND OF NOD

FROM breakfast on through all the day
At home among my friends I stay;
But every night I go abroad
Afar into the land of Nod.

All by myself I have to go,
With none to tell me what to do—
All alone beside the streams
And up the mountain-sides of dreams.

The strangest things are there for me,
Both things to eat and things to see
And many frightening sights abroad
Till morning in the land of Nod.

Try as I like to find the way,
I never can get back by day,
Nor can remember plain and clear
The curious music that I hear.

XVIII

MY SHADOW

I HAVE a little shadow that goes in and out with me,
And what can be the use of him is more than I can
see.
He is very, very like me from the heels up to the
head;
And I see him jump before me, when I jump into my
bed.

The funniest thing about him is the way he likes to
grow—
Not at all like proper children, which is always very
slow;

For he sometimes shoots up taller like an india rub-
ber ball,
And he sometimes gets so little that there's none of
him at all.

He hasn't got a notion of how children ought to play,
And can only make a fool of me in every sort of way.
He stays so close beside me, he's a coward you can
see;
I'd think shame to stick to nursie as that shadow
sticks to me!

One morning, very early, before the sun was up,
I rose and found the shining dew on every buttercup;
But my lazy little shadow, like an arrant sleepy-head,
Had stayed at home behind me and was fast asleep
in bed.

XIX

SYSTEM

EVERY night my prayers I say,
And get my dinner every day;
And every day that I've been good,
I get an orange after food.

The child that is not clean and neat,
With lots of toys and things to eat,
He is a naughty child, I'm sure—
Or else his dear papa is poor.

XX

A GOOD BOY

I WOKE before the morning, I was happy all the
day,
I never said an ugly word, but smiled and stuck to
play.

And now at last the sun is going down behind the
wood,
And I am very happy, for I know that I've been
good.

My bed is waiting cool and fresh, with linen smooth
and fair,
And I must off to sleepsin-by, and not forget my
prayer.

I know that, till to-morrow I shall see the sun arise,
No ugly dream shall fright my mind, no ugly sight
my eyes,
But slumber hold me tightly till I waken in the dawn,
And hear the thrushes singing in the lilacs round the
lawn.

XXI

ESCAPE AT BEDTIME

THE lights from the parlor and kitchen shone out
   Through the blinds and the windows and bars;
And high overhead and all moving about,
   There were thousands of millions of stars.
There ne'er were such thousands of leaves on a tree,
   Nor of people in church or the Park,
As the crowds of the stars that looked down upon me,
   And that glittered and winked in the dark.

The Dog, and the Plow, and the Hunter, and all,
   And the star of the sailor, and Mars,
These shone in the sky, and the pail by the wall
   Would be half full of water and stars.
They saw me at last, and they chased me with cries,
   And they soon had me packed into bed;
But the glory kept shining and bright in my eyes,
   And the stars going round in my head.

XXII

MARCHING SONG

BRING the comb and play upon it!
   Marching, here we come!
Willie cocks his highland bonnet,
   Johnnie beats the drum.

Mary Jane commands the party,
    Peter leads the rear;
Feet in time, alert and hearty,
    Each a Grenadier!

All in the most martial manner
    Marching double-quick;
While the napkin like a banner
    Waves upon the stick!

Here's enough of fame and pillage,
    Great commander Jane!
Now that we've been round the village,
    Let's go home again.

XXIII

THE COW

THE friendly cow all red and white,
    I love with all my heart:
She gives me cream with all her might,
    To eat with apple-tart.

She wanders lowing here and there,
    And yet she cannot stray,
All in the pleasant open air,
    The pleasant light of day;

And blown by all the winds that pass
    And wet with all the showers,
She walks among the meadow grass
    And eats the meadow flowers.

XXIV

HAPPY THOUGHT

THE world is so full of a number of things,
I'm sure we should all be as happy as kings.

XXV

THE WIND

I SAW you toss the kites on high
And blow the birds about the sky;
And all around I heard you pass,
Like ladies' skirts across the grass—
    O wind, a-blowing all day long,
    O wind, that sings so loud a song!

I saw the different things you did,
But always you yourself you hid,
I felt you push, I heard you call,
I could not see yourself at all—
    O wind, a-blowing all day long,
    O wind, that sings so loud a song!

O you that are so strong and cold,
O blower, are you young or old?
Are you a beast of field and tree,
Or just a stronger child than me?
    O wind, a-blowing all day long,
    O wind, that sings so loud a song!

XXVI

KEEPSAKE MILL

OVER the borders, a sin without pardon,
   Breaking the branches and crawling below,
Out through the breach in the wall of the garden,
   Down by the banks of the river, we go.

Here is the mill with the humming of thunder,
   Here is the weir with the wonder of foam,
Here is the sluice with the race running under—
   Marvelous places, though handy to home!

Sounds of the village grow stiller and stiller,
   Stiller the notes of the birds on the hill;
Dusty and dim are the eyes of the miller,
   Deaf are his ears with the moil of the mill.

Years may go by, and the wheel in the river
   Wheels as it wheels for us, children, to-day,
Wheel and keep roaring and foaming forever
   Long after all of the boys are away.

Home from the Indies and home from the ocean,
   Heroes and soldiers we all shall come home;
Still we shall find the old mill-wheel in motion,
   Turning and churning that river to foam.

You with the bean that I gave when we quarreled,
   I with your marble of Saturday last,
Honored and old and all gayly appareled,
   Here we shall meet and remember the past.

XXVII

GOOD AND BAD CHILDREN

CHILDREN, you are very little,
And your bones are very brittle;
If you would grow great and stately,
You must try to walk sedately.

You must still be bright and quiet,
And content with simple diet;
And remain through all bewild'ring,
Innocent and honest children.

Happy hearts and happy faces,
Happy play in grassy places—
That was how in ancient ages,
Children grew to kings and sages.

But the unkind and the unruly,
And the sort who eat unduly,
They must never hope for glory—
Theirs is quite a different story!

Cruel children, crying babies,
All grow up as geese and gabies,
Hated, as their age increases,
By their nephews and their nieces.

XXVIII

FOREIGN CHILDREN

LITTLE Indian, Sioux or Crow,
Little frosty Eskimo,
Little Turk or Japanee,
O! don't you wish that you were me?

You have seen the scarlet trees
And the lions over seas;
You have eaten ostrich eggs,
And turned the turtles off their legs.

Such a life is very fine,
But it's not so nice as mine:
You must often, as you trod,
Have wearied *not* to be abroad.

You have curious things to eat,
I am fed on proper meat;
You must dwell beyond the foam,
But I am safe and live at home.

Little Indian, Sioux or Crow,
Little frosty Eskimo,
Little Turk or Japanee,
O! don't you wish that you were me?

XXIX

THE SUN'S TRAVELS

THE sun is not a-bed, when I
At night upon my pillow lie;
Still round the earth his way he takes,
And morning after morning makes.

While here at home, in shining day,
We round the sunny garden play,
Each little Indian sleepy-head
Is being kissed and put to bed.

And when at eve I rise from tea,
Day dawns beyond the Atlantic Sea,
And all the children in the West
Are getting up and being dressed.

XXX

THE LAMPLIGHTER

MY tea is nearly ready and the sun has left the sky;
It's time to take the window to see Leerie going by;
For every night at teatime and before you take your
  seat,
With lantern and with ladder he comes posting up
  the street.

Now Tom would be a driver and Maria go to sea,
And my papa's a banker and as rich as he can be;

But I, when I am stronger and can choose what I'm
    to do,
O Leerie, I'll go round at night and light the lamps
    with you.

For we are very lucky, with a lamp before the door,
And Leerie stops to light it as he lights so many
    more;
And O! before you hurry by with ladder and with
    light,
O Leerie, see a little child and nod to him to-night!

XXXI

MY BED IS A BOAT

MY bed is like a little boat;
    Nurse helps me in when I embark;
She girds me in my sailor's coat
    And starts me in the dark.

At night I go on board and say
    Good-night to all my friends in shore;
I shut my eyes and sail away
    And see and hear no more.

And sometimes things to bed I take,
    As prudent sailors have to do:
Perhaps a slice of wedding-cake,
    Perhaps a toy or two.

All night across the dark we steer:
  But when the day returns at last,
Safe in my room beside the pier,
  I find my vessel fast.

XXXII

THE MOON

THE moon has a face like the clock in the hall;
She shines on thieves on the garden wall,
On streets and fields and harbor quays,
And birdies asleep in the forks of the trees.

The squalling cat and the squeaking mouse,
The howling dog by the door of the house,
The bat that lies in bed at noon,
All love to be out by the light of the moon.

But all of the things that belong to the day
Cuddle to sleep to be out of her way;
And flowers and children close their eyes
Till up in the morning the sun shall arise.

XXXIII

THE SWING

HOW do you like to go up in a swing,
  Up in the air so blue?
Oh, I do think it the pleasantest thing
  Ever a child can do!

Up in the air and over the wall,
  Till I can see so wide,
Rivers and trees and cattle and all
  Over the countryside—

Till I look down on the garden green
  Down on the roof so brown—
Up in the air I go flying again,
  Up in the air and down!

XXXIV

TIME TO RISE

A BIRDIE with a yellow bill
Hopped upon the window-sill,
Cocked his shining eye and said:
"Ain't you 'shamed, you sleepy-head?"

XXXV

LOOKING-GLASS RIVER

SMOOTH it slides upon its travel,
  Here a wimple, there a gleam—
    O the clean gravel!
    O the smooth stream!

Sailing blossoms, silver fishes,
  Paven pools as clear as air—
    How a child wishes
    To live down there!

We can see our colored faces
  Floating on the shaken pool
    Down in cool places,
    Dim and very cool;

Till a wind or water wrinkle,
  Dipping martin, plumping trout,
    Spreads in a twinkle
    And blots all out.

See the rings pursue each other;
  All below grows black as night,
    Just as if mother
    Had blown out the light!

Patience, children, just a minute—
  See the spreading circles die;
    The stream and all in it
    Will clear by-and-by.

XXXVI

FAIRY BREAD

COME up here, O dusty feet!
Here is fairy bread to eat.
Here is my retiring room,
  Children, you may dine
On the golden smell of broom
  And the shade of pine;
And when you have eaten well,
Fairy stories hear and tell.

XXXVII

FROM A RAILWAY CARRIAGE

FASTER than fairies, faster than witches,
Bridges and houses, hedges and ditches;
And charging along like troops in a battle,
All through the meadows the horses and cattle:
All of the sights of the hill and the plain
Fly as thick as driving rain;
And ever again in the wink of an eye,
Painted stations whistle by.
Here is a child who clambers and scrambles,
All by himself and gathering brambles;
Here is a tramp who stands and gazes;
And there is the green for stringing the daisies!
Here is a cart run away in the road
Lumping along with man and load;
And here is a mill and there is a river:
Each a glimpse and gone forever!

XXXVIII

WINTER-TIME

LATE lies the wintry sun a-bed,
A frosty, fiery sleepy-head;
Blinks but an hour or two; and then,
A blood-red orange, sets again.

Before the stars have left the skies,
At morning in the dark I rise;
And shivering in my nakedness,
By the cold candle, bathe and dress.

Close by the jolly fire I sit
To warm my frozen bones a bit;
Or with a reindeer-sled explore
The colder countries round the door.

When to go out my nurse doth wrap
Me in my comforter and cap:
The cold wind burns my face, and blows
Its frosty pepper up my nose.

Black are my steps on silver sod;
Thick blows my frosty breath abroad;
And tree and house, and hill and lake,
Are frosted like a wedding-cake.

XXXIX

THE HAYLOFT

THROUGH all the pleasant meadow-side
    The grass grew shoulder-high,
Till the shining scythes went far and wide
    And cut it down to dry.

These green and sweetly-smelling crops
    They led in wagons home:
And they piled them here in mountain-tops
    For mountaineers to roam.

Here is Mount Clear, Mount Rusty Nail,
  Mount Eagle and Mount High;—
The mice that in these mountains dwell,
  No happier are than I!

O what a joy to clamber there,
  O what a place for play,
With the sweet, the dim, the dusty air,
  The happy hills of hay.

XL

FAREWELL TO THE FARM

THE coach is at the door at last;
The eager children mounting fast
And kissing hands, in chorus sing:
Good-by, good-by, to everything!

To house and garden, field and lawn,
The meadow-gates we swung upon,
To pump and stable, tree and swing,
Good-by, good-by, to everything!

And fare you well for evermore,
O ladder at the hayloft door,
O hayloft where the cobwebs cling,
Good-by, good-by, to everything!

Crack goes the whip, and off we go;
The trees and houses smaller grow;
Last, round the woody turn we swing:
Good-by, good-by, to everything!

XLI

NORTH-WEST PASSAGE

1. *Good-Night*

WHEN the bright lamp is carried in,
The sunless hours again begin;
O'er all without, in field and lane,
The haunted night returns again.

Now we behold the embers flee
About the firelit hearth; and see
Our faces painted as we pass,
Like pictures, on the window-glass.

Must we to bed indeed? Well then,
Let us arise and go like men,
And face with an undaunted tread
The long black passage up to bed.

Farewell, O brother, sister, sire!
O pleasant party round the fire!
The songs you sing, the tales you tell,
Till far to-morrow, fare ye well!

2. *Shadow March*

All round the house is the jet-black night;
    It stares through the window-pane;
It crawls in the corners, hiding from the light,
    And it moves with the moving flame.

Now my little heart goes a-beating like a drum,
   With the breath of the Bogie in my hair;
And all round the candle the crooked shadows come
   And go marching along up the stair.

The shadow of the balusters, the shadow of the lamp,
   The shadow of the child that goes to bed—
All the wicked shadows coming, tramp, tramp,
   tramp,
   With the black night overhead.

3. In Port

Last, to the chamber where I lie
My fearful footsteps patter nigh,
And come from out the cold and gloom
Into my warm and cheerful room.

There, safe arrived, we turn about
To keep the coming shadows out,
And close the happy door at last
On all the perils that we past.

Then, when mamma goes by to bed.
She shall come in with tiptoe tread,
And see me lying warm and fast
And in the Land of Nod at last.

THE CHILD ALONE

I

THE UNSEEN PLAYMATE

WHEN children are playing alone on the green,
In comes the playmate that never was seen.
When children are happy and lonely and good,
The Friend of the Children comes out of the wood.

Nobody heard him and nobody saw,
His is a picture you never could draw,
But he's sure to be present, abroad or at home,
When children are happy and playing alone.

He lies in the laurels, he runs on the grass,
He sings when you tinkle the musical glass;
Whene'er you are happy and cannot tell why,
The Friend of the Children is sure to be by!

He loves to be little, he hates to be big,
'Tis he that inhabits the caves that you dig;
'Tis he when you play with your soldiers of tin
That sides with the Frenchmen and never can win.

'Tis he when at night you go off to your bed,
Bids you go to your sleep and not trouble your head;
For wherever they're lying, in cupboard or shelf,
'Tis he will take care of your playthings himself!

II

MY SHIP AND I

O IT'S I that am the captain of a tidy little ship,
  Of a ship that goes a-sailing on the pond;
And my ship it keeps a-turning all around and all
    about;
But when I'm a little older, I shall find the secret out
  How to send my vessel sailing on beyond.

For I mean to grow as little as the dolly at the helm,
  And the dolly I intend to come alive;
And with him beside to help me, it's a-sailing I
    shall go,
It's a-sailing on the water, where the jolly breezes
    blow
  And the vessel goes a divie-divie-dive.

O it's then you'll see me sailing through the rushes
    and the reeds,
  And you'll hear the water singing at the prow;
For beside the dolly sailor I'm to voyage and ex-
    plore,
To land upon the island where no dolly was before,
  And to fire the penny cannon in the bow.

III

MY KINGDOM

DOWN by a shining water well
I found a very little dell,
   No higher than my head.
The heather and the gorse about
In summer bloom were coming out,
   Some yellow and some red.

I called the little pool a sea;
The little hills were big to me;
   For I am very small.
I made a boat, I made a town,
I searched the caverns up and down,
   And named them one and all.

And all about was mine, I said,
The little sparrows overhead,
   The little minnows too.
This was the world and I was king;
For me the bees came by to sing,
   For me the swallows flew.

I played there were no deeper seas,
Nor any wider plains than these,
   Nor other kings than me.
At last I heard my mother call
Out from the house at evenfall,
   To call me home to tea.

And I must rise and leave my dell,
And leave my dimpled water well,
      And leave my heather blooms!
Alas! and as my home I neared
How very big my nurse appeared,
      How great and cool the rooms!

IV

PICTURE BOOKS IN WINTER

SUMMER fading, winter comes—
Frosty mornings, tingling thumbs,
Window robins, winter rooks,
And the picture story-books.

Water now is turned to stone
Nurse and I can walk upon;
Still we find the flowing brooks
In the picture story-books.

All the pretty things put by,
Wait upon the children's eye,
Sheep and shepherds, trees and crooks,
In the picture story-books.

We may see how all things are,
Seas and cities, near and far,
And the flying fairies' looks,
In the picture story-books.

How am I to sing your praise,
Happy chimney-corner days,
Sitting safe in nursery nooks,
Reading picture story-books?

V

MY TREASURES

THESE nuts that I keep in the back of the nest
Where all my lead soldiers are lying at rest,
Were gathered in autumn by nursie and me
In a wood with a well by the side of the sea.

This whistle we made (and how clearly it sounds!)
By the side of a field at the end of the grounds.
Of a branch of a plane, with a knife of my own,
It was nursie who made it, and nursie alone!

The stone, with the white and the yellow and gray,
We discovered I cannot tell how far away;
And I carried it back, although weary and cold,
For though father denies it, I'm sure it is gold.

But of all of my treasures the last is the king,
For there's very few children possess such a thing;
And that is a chisel, both handle and blade,
Which a man who was really a carpenter made.

VI

BLOCK CITY

WHAT are you able to build with your blocks?
Castles and palaces, temples and docks.
Rain may keep raining, and others go roam,
But I can be happy and building at home.

Let the sofa be mountains, the carpet be sea,
There I'll establish a city for me:
A kirk and a mill and a palace beside,
And a harbor as well where my vessels may ride,

Great is the palace with pillar and wall,
A sort of a tower on the top of it all,
And steps coming down in an orderly way,
To where my toy vessels lie safe in the bay.

This one is sailing and that one is moored:
Hark to the song of the sailors on board!
And see on the steps of my palace the kings
Coming and going with presents and things!

Now I have done with it, down let it go!
All in a moment the town is laid low.
Block upon block lying scattered and free,
What is there left of my town by the sea?

Yet as I saw it, I see it again,
The kirk and the palace, the ships and the men,
And as long as I live and where'er I may be,
I'll always remember my town by the sea.

VII

THE LAND OF STORY BOOKS

AT evening when the lamp is lit,
Around the fire my parents sit;
They sit at home and talk and sing,
And do not play at anything.

Now, with my little gun, I crawl
All in the dark along the wall,
And follow round the forest track
Away behind the sofa back.

There, in the night, where none can spy,
All in my hunter's camp I lie,
And play at books that I have read
Till it is time to go to bed.

These are the hills, these are the woods,
These are my starry solitudes;
And there the river by whose brink
The roaring lions come to drink.

I see the others far away
As if in firelit camp they lay,
And I, like to an Indian scout,
Around their party prowled about.

So, when my nurse comes in for me,
Home I return across the sea,
And go to bed with backward looks
At my dear land of Story-books.

VIII

ARMIES IN THE FIRE

THE lamps now glitter down the street;
Faintly sound the falling feet;
And the blue even slowly falls
About the garden trees and walls.

Now in the falling of the gloom
The red fire paints the empty room:
And warmly on the roof it looks,
And flickers on the backs of books.

Armies march by tower and spire
Of cities blazing, in the fire;—
Till as I gaze with staring eyes,
The armies fade, the luster dies.

Then once again the glow returns;
Again the phantom city burns;
And down the red-hot valley, lo!
The phantom armies marching go!

Blinking embers, tell me true
Where are those armies marching to,
And what the burning city is
That crumbles in your furnaces!

IX

THE LITTLE LAND

WHEN at home alone I sit
And am very tired of it,
I have just to shut my eyes
To go sailing through the skies—
To go sailing far away
To the pleasant Land of Play;
To the fairy land afar
Where the Little People are;
Where the clover-tops are trees,
And the rain-pools are the seas,
And the leaves like little ships
Sail about on tiny trips;
And above the daisy tree
      Through the grasses
High o'erhead the Bumble Bee
      Hums and passes.

In that forest to and fro
I can wander, I can go;
See the spider and the fly,
And the ants go marching by
Carrying parcels with their feet
Down the green and grassy street.
I can in the sorrel sit
Where the ladybird alit.

I can climb the jointed grass;
    And on high
See the greater swallows pass
    In the sky,
And the round sun rolling by
Heeding no such things as I.

Through that forest I can pass
Till, as in a looking-glass,
Humming fly and daisy tree
And my tiny self I see,
Painted very clear and neat
On the rain-pool at my feet.
Should a leaflet come to land
Drifting near to where I stand,
Straight I'll board that tiny boat
Round the rain-pool sea to float.

Little thoughtful creatures sit
On the grassy coasts of it;
Little things with lovely eyes
See me sailing with surprise.
Some are clad in armor green—
(These have sure to battle been!)—
Some are pied with every hue,
Black and crimson, gold and blue;
Some have wings and swift are gone;—
But they all look kindly on.

When my eyes I once again
Open, and see all things plain:

High bare walls, great bare floor;
Great big knobs on drawer and door;
Great big people perched on chairs,
Stitching tucks and mending tears,
Each a hill that I could climb,
And talking nonsense all the time—
    O dear me,
    That I could be
A sailor on the rain-pool sea,
A climber in the clover tree,
And just come back, a sleepy-head,
Late at night to go to bed.

GARDEN DAYS

I

NIGHT AND DAY

WHEN the golden day is done,
  Through the closing portal,
Child and garden, flower and sun,
  Vanish all things mortal.

As the blinding shadows fall,
  As the rays diminish,
Under evening's cloak, they all
  Roll away and vanish.

Garden darkened, daisy shut,
  Child in bed, they slumber—
Glow-worm in the highway rut,
  Mice among the lumber.

In the darkness houses shine,
  Parents move with candles;
Till on all the night divine
  Turns the bedroom handles.

Till at last the day begins
  In the east a-breaking,
In the hedges and the whins
  Sleeping birds a-waking.

In the darkness shapes of things,
   Houses, trees, and hedges,
Clearer grow: and sparrows' wings
   Beat on window ledges.

These shall wake the yawning maid;
   She the door shall open—
Finding dew on garden glade
   And the morning broken.

There my garden grows again
   Green and rosy painted,
As at eve behind the pane
   From my eyes it fainted.

Just as it was shut away,
   Toy-like in the even,
Here I see it glow with day
   Under glowing heaven.

Every path and every plot,
   Every bush of roses,
Every blue forget-me-not
   Where the dew reposes,

"Up!" they cry, "the day is come
   On the smiling valleys:
We have beat the morning drum;
   Playmate, join your allies!"

II

NEST EGGS

BIRDS all the sunny day
  Flutter and quarrel
Here in the arbor-like
  Tent of the laurel.

Here in the fork
  The brown nest is seated;
Four little blue eggs
  The mother keeps heated.

While we stand watching her,
  Staring like gabies,
Safe in each egg are the
  Bird's little babies.

Soon the frail eggs they shall
  Chip, and upspringing
Make all the April woods
  Merry with singing.

Younger than we are,
  O children, and frailer,
Soon in blue air they'll be,
  Singer and sailor.

We so much older,
  Taller and stronger,
We shall look down on the
  Birdies no longer.

They shall go flying
  With musical speeches
High overhead in the
  Tops of the beeches.

In spite of our wisdom
  And sensible talking,
We on our feet must go
  Plodding and walking.

III

THE FLOWERS

ALL the names I know from nurse:
Gardener's garters, Shepherd's purse,
Bachelor's buttons, Lady's smock,
And the Lady Hollyhock.

Fairy places, fairy things,
Fairy woods where the wild bee wings,
Tiny trees for tiny dames—
These must all be fairy names!

Tiny woods below whose boughs
Shady fairies weave a house;
Tiny tree-tops, rose or thyme,
Where the braver fairies climb!

Fair are grown-up people's trees,
But the fairest woods are these;
Where if I were not so tall,
I should live for good and all.

IV

SUMMER SUN

GREAT is the sun, and wide he goes
Through empty heaven without repose;
And in the blue and glowing days
More thick than rain he showers his rays.

Though closer still the blinds we pull
To keep the shady parlor cool,
Yet he will find a chink or two
To slip his golden fingers through.

The dusty attic, spider-clad,
He through the key-hole maketh glad;
And through the broken edge of tiles,
Into the laddered hayloft smiles.

Meantime his golden face around
He bares to all the garden ground,
And sheds a warm and glittering look
Among the ivy's inmost nook.

Above the hills, along the blue,
Round the bright air with footing true,
To please the child, to paint the rose,
The gardener of the World, he goes.

V

THE DUMB SOLDIER

WHEN the grass was closely mown,
Walking on the lawn alone,
In the turf a hole I found
And hid a soldier underground.

Spring and daisies came apace;
Grasses hide my hiding-place;
Grasses run like a green sea
O'er the lawn up to my knee.

Under grass alone he lies,
Looking up with leaden eyes,
Scarlet coat and pointed gun,
To the stars and to the sun.

When the grass is ripe like grain,
When the scythe is stoned again,
When the lawn is shaven clear,
Then my hole shall reappear.

I shall find him, never fear,
I shall find my grenadier;
But for all that's gone and come,
I shall find my soldier dumb.

He has lived, a little thing,
In the grassy woods of spring;
Done, if he could tell me true
Just as I should like to do.

He has seen the starry hours
And the springing of the flowers;
And the fairy things that pass
In the forests of the grass.

In the silence he has heard
Talking bee and ladybird,
And the butterfly has flown,
O'er him as he lay alone.

Not a word will he disclose,
Not a word of all he knows.
I must lay him on the shelf,
And make up the tale myself.

VI

AUTUMN FIRES

IN the other gardens
    And all up the vale,
From the autumn bonfires
    See the smoke trail!

Pleasant summer over
    And all the summer flowers,
The red fire blazes,
    The gray smoke towers.

Sing a song of seasons!
    Something bright in all!
Flowers in the summer,
    Fires in the fall!

VII

THE GARDENER

THE gardener does not love to talk,
He makes me keep the gravel walk;
And when he puts his tools away,
He locks the door and takes the key.

Away behind the currant row
Where no one else but cook may go,
Far in the plots, I see him dig,
Old and serious, brown and big.

He digs the flowers, green, red, and blue,
Nor wishes to be spoken to.
He digs the flowers and cuts the hay,
And never seems to want to play.

Silly gardener! summer goes,
And winter comes with pinching toes.
When in the garden bare and brown
You must lay your barrow down.

Well now, and while the summer stays,
To profit by these garden days,
O how much wiser you would be
To play at Indian wars with me!

VIII

HISTORICAL ASSOCIATIONS

DEAR Uncle Jim, this garden ground
That now you smoke your pipe around,
Has seen immortal actions done
And valiant battles lost and won.

Here we had best on tip-toe tread,
While I for safety march ahead,
For this is that enchanted ground
Where all who loiter slumber sound.

Here is the sea, here is the sand,
Here is simple Shepherd's Land,
Here are the fairy hollyhocks,
And there are Ali Baba's rocks.

But yonder, see! apart and high,
Frozen Siberia lies; where I,
With Robert Bruce and William Tell,
Was bound by an enchanter's spell.

There, then, awhile in chains we lay,
In wintry dungeons, far from day;
But ris'n at length, with might and main,
Our iron fetters burst in twain.

Then all the horns were blown in town;
And to the ramparts clanging down,

All the giants leaped to horse
And charged behind us through the gorse.

On we rode, the others and I,
Over the mountains blue, and by
The Silver River, the sounding sea,
And the robber woods of Tartary.

A thousand miles we galloped fast,
And down the witches' lane we passed,
And rode amain, with brandished sword,
Up to the middle, through the ford.

Last we drew rein—a weary three—
Upon the lawn, in time for tea,
And from our steeds alighted down
Before the gates of Babylon.

ENVOYS

I

TO WILLIE AND HENRIETTA

IF two may read aright
These rhymes of old delight
And house and garden play,
You two, my cousins, and you only, may.

You in a garden green
With me were king and queen,
Were hunter, soldier, tar,
And all the thousand things that children are.

Now in the elders' seat
We rest with quiet feet,
And from the window-bay
We watch the children, our successors, play.

"Time was," the golden head
Irrevocably said;
But time which none can bind,
While flowing fast away, leaves love behind.

II

TO MY MOTHER

YOU too, my mother, read my rhymes
For love of unforgotten times,
And you may chance to hear once more
The little feet along the floor.

III

TO AUNTIE

CHIEF of our aunts—not only I,
But all your dozen of nurslings cry—
What did the other children do?
And what were childhood, wanting you?

IV

TO MINNIE

THE red room with the giant bed
Where none but elders laid their head;
The little room where you and I
Did for a while together lie
And, simple suitor, I your hand
In decent marriage did demand;
The great day nursery, best of all,
With pictures pasted on the wall
And leaves upon the blind—

A pleasant room wherein to wake
And hear the leafy garden shake
And rustle in the wind—
And pleasant there to lie in bed
And see the pictures overhead—
The wars about Sebastopol,
The grinning guns along the wall,
The daring escalade,
The plunging ships, the bleating sheep,
The happy children ankle-deep
And laughing as they wade:
All these are vanished clean away,
And the old manse is changed to-day;
It wears an altered face
And shields a stranger race.
The river, on from mill to mill,
Flows past our childhood's garden still;
But ah! we children nevermore
Shall watch it from the water-door!
Below the yew—it still is there—
Our phantom voices haunt the air
As we were still at play,
And I can hear them call and say:
"How far is it to Babylon?"

Ah, far enough, my dear,
Far, far enough from here—
Yet you have further gone!
"Can I get there by candle-light?"
So goes the old refrain.

I do not know—perchance you might—
But only, children, hear it right,
Ah, never to return again!
The eternal dawn, beyond a doubt,
Shall break on hill and plain,
And put all stars and candles out,
Ere we be young again.

To you in distant India, these
I send across the seas,
Nor count it far across.
For which of us forgets
The Indian cabinets,
The bones of antelope, the wings of albatross,
The pied and painted birds and beans,
The junks and bangles, beads and screens,
The gods and sacred bells,
And the loud-humming, twisted shells?
The level of the parlor floor
Was honest, homely, Scottish shore;
But when we climbed upon a chair,
Behold the gorgeous East was there!

Be this a fable; and behold
Me in the parlor as of old,
And Minnie just above me set
In the quaint Indian cabinet!
Smiling and kind, you grace a shelf
Too high for me to reach myself.
Reach down a hand, my dear, and take
These rhymes for old acquaintance's sake.

V

TO MY NAME-CHILD

1

SOME day soon this rhyming volume, if you learn
  with proper speed,
Little Louis Sanchez, will be given you to read.
Then shall you discover, that your name was printed
  down
By the English printers, long before, in London
  town.
In the great and busy city where the East and West
  are met,
All the little letters did the English printer set;
While you thought of nothing, and were still too
  young to play,
Foreign people thought of you in places far away.

Ay, and while you slept, a baby, over all the English
  lands
Other little children took the volume in their hands;
Other children questioned, in their homes across the
  seas:
Who was little Louis, won't you tell us, mother,
  please?

2

Now that you have spelt your lesson, lay it down and
  go and play,
Seeking shells and seaweed on the sands of Monte-
  rey

Watching all the mighty whalebones, lying buried
    by the breeze,
Tiny sandy-pipers, and the huge Pacific seas.
And remember in your playing, as the sea-fog rolls
    to you,
Long ere you could read it, how I told you what
    to do;
And that while you thought of no one, nearly half
    the world away
Some one thought of Louis on the beach of Monte-
    rey!

VI

TO ANY READER

AS from the house your mother sees
You playing round the garden trees,
So you may see, if you will look
Through the windows of this book,
Another child, far, far away,
And in another garden, play.
But do not think you can at all,
By knocking on the window, call
That child to hear you. He intent
Is all on his play-business bent.
He does not hear; he will not look,
Nor yet be lured out of this book.
For, long ago, the truth to say,
He has grown up and gone away,
And it is but a child of air
That lingers in the garden there.

UNDERWOODS

BOOK I: IN ENGLISH

I

ENVOY

GO, little book, and wish to all
Flowers in the garden, meat in the hall,
A bin of wine, a spice of wit,
A house with lawns inclosing it,
A living river by the door,
A nightingale in the sycamore!

II

A SONG OF THE ROAD

THE gauger walked with willing foot,
And aye the gauger played the flute;
And what should Master Gauger play
But *Over the hills and far away?*

Whene'er I buckle on my pack
And foot it gayly in the track,
O pleasant gauger, long since dead,
I hear you fluting on ahead.

You go with me the self-same way—
The self-same air for me you play;

For I do think and so do you
It is the tune to travel to.

For who would gravely set his face
To go to this or t'other place?
There's nothing under heav'n so blue
That's fairly worth the traveling to.

On every hand the roads begin,
And people walk with zeal therein;
But wheresoe'er the highways tend,
Be sure there's nothing at the end.

Then follow you, wherever hie
The traveling mountains of the sky.
Or let the streams in civil mode
Direct your choice upon a road;

For one and all, or high or low,
Will lead you where you wish to go;
And one and all go night and day
Over the hills and far away!

Forest of Montargis, 1878.

III

THE CANOE SPEAKS

ON the great streams the ships may go
About men's business to and fro.
But I, the egg-shell pinnace, sleep
On crystal waters ankle-deep:
I, whose diminutive design,
Of sweeter cedar, pithier pine,

Is fashioned on so frail a mold,
A hand may launch, a hand withhold:
I, rather, with the leaping trout
Wind, among lilies, in and out;
I, the unnamed, inviolate,
Green, rustic rivers navigate;
My dipping paddle scarcely shakes
The berry in the bramble-brakes;
Still forth on my green way I wend
Beside the cottage garden-end;
And by the nested angler fare,
And take the lovers unaware.
By willow wood and water-wheel
Speedily fleets my touching keel;
By all retired and shady spots
Where prosper dim forget-me-nots;
By meadows where at afternoon
The growing maidens troop in June
To loose their girdles on the grass.
Ah! speedier than before the glass
The backward toilet goes; and swift
As swallows quiver, robe and shift
And the rough country stockings lie
Around each young divinity.
When, following the recondite brook,
Sudden upon this scene I look,
And light with unfamiliar face
On chaste Diana's bathing-place,
Loud ring the hills about and all
The shallows are abandoned. . . .

IV

IT is the season now to go
About the country high and low,
Among the lilacs hand in hand,
And two by two in fairy land.

The brooding boy, the sighing maid,
Wholly fain and half afraid,
Now meet along the hazel'd brook
To pass and linger, pause and look.

A year ago, and blithely paired,
Their rough-and-tumble play they shared;
They kissed and quarreled, laughed and cried,
A year ago at Eastertide.

With bursting heart, with fiery face,
She strove against him in the race;
He, unabashed, her garter saw,
That now would touch her skirts with awe.

Now by the stile ablaze she stops,
And his demurer eyes he drops;
Now they exchange averted sighs
Or stand and marry silent eyes.

And he to her a hero is,
And sweeter she than primroses;
Their common silence dearer far
Than nightingale and mavis are.

Now when they sever wedded hands,
Joy trembles in their bosom-strands,
And lovely laughter leaps and falls
Upon their lips in madrigals.

V

THE HOUSE BEAUTIFUL

A NAKED house, a naked moor,
A shivering pool before the door,
A garden bare of flowers and fruit,
And poplars at the garden foot:
Such is the place that I live in,
Bleak without and bare within.
Yet shall your ragged moor receive
The incomparable pomp of eve,
And the cold glories of the dawn
Behind your shivering trees be drawn;
And when the wind from place to place
Doth the unmoored cloud-galleons chase,
Your garden gloom and gleam again,
With leaping sun, with glancing rain.
Here shall the wizard moon ascend
The heavens, in the crimson end
Of day's declining splendor; here
The army of the stars appear.
The neighbor hollows dry or wet,
Spring shall with tender flowers beset;
And oft the morning muser see
Larks rising from the broomy lea,

And every fairy wheel and thread
Of cobweb dew-bediamoned.
When daisies go, shall winter time
Silver the simple grass with rime;
Autumnal frosts enchant the pool
And make the cart-ruts beautiful;
And when snow-bright the moor expands
How shall your children clap their hands!
To make this earth our hermitage,
A cheerful and a changeful page.
God's bright and intricate device
Of days and seasons doth suffice.

VI

A VISIT FROM THE SEA

FAR from the loud sea beaches
  Where he goes fishing and crying,
Here in the inland garden
  Why is the sea-gull flying?

Here are no fish to dive for;
  Here is the corn and lea;
Here are the green trees rustling.
  Hie away home to sea!

Fresh is the river water
  And quiet among the rushes;
This is no home for the sea-gull
  But for the rooks and thrushes.

Pity the bird that has wandered!
   Pity the sailor ashore!
Hurry him home to the ocean,
   Let him come here no more.

High on the sea-cliff ledges
   The white gulls are trooping and crying
Here among rooks and roses,
   Why is the sea-gull flying?

VII

TO A GARDENER

FRIEND, in my mountain side demesne,
My plain-beholding, rosy, green
And linnet-haunted garden-ground,
Let still the esculents abound.
Let first the onion flourish there,
Rose among roots, the maiden-fair,
Wine-scented and poetic soul
Of the capacious salad bowl.
Let thyme the mountaineer (to dress
The tinier birds) and wading cress,
The lover of the shallow brook,
From all my plots and borders look.

Nor crisp and ruddy radish, nor
Pease-cods for the child's pinafore
Be lacking; nor of salad clan
The last and least that ever ran

About great nature's garden-beds.
Nor thence be missed the speary heads
Of artichoke; nor thence the bean
That gathered innocent and green
Outsavors the belauded pea.

These tend, I prithee; and for me,
Thy most long-suffering master, bring
In April, when the linnets sing
And the days lengthen more and more
At sundown to the garden door.
And I, being provided thus,
Shall, with superb asparagus,
A book, a taper, and a cup
Of country wine, divinely sup.

La Solitude, Hyères.

VIII

TO MINNIE

(*With a Hand-Glass*)

A PICTURE-FRAME for you to fill,
  A paltry setting for your face,
A thing that has no worth until
  You lend it something of your grace,

I send (unhappy I that sing
  Laid by a while upon the shelf)
Because I would not send a thing
  Less charming than you are yourself.

And happier than I, alas!
  (Dumb thing, I envy its delight),
'Twill wish you well, the looking-glass,
  And look you in the face to-night.

1869.

IX

TO K. DE M.

A LOVER of the moorland bare
And honest country winds, you were;
The silver-skimming rain you took;
And loved the floodings of the brook,
Dew, frost and mountains, fire and seas,
Tumultuary silences,
Winds that in darkness fifed a tune,
And the high-riding virgin moon.

And as the berry, pale and sharp,
Springs on some ditch's counterscarp
In our ungenial, native north—
You put your frosted wildings forth,
And on the heath, afar from man,
A strong and bitter virgin ran.

The berry ripened keeps the rude
And racy flavor of the wood;
And you that loved the empty plain
All redolent of wind and rain,
Around you still the curlew sings—

The freshness of the weather clings—
The maiden jewels of the rain
Sit in your dabbled locks again.

X

TO N. V. DE G. S.

THE unfathomable sea, and time, and tears,
The deeds of heroes and the crimes of kings
Dispart us; and the river of events
Has, for an age of years, to east and west
More widely borne our cradles. Thou to me
Art foreign, as when seamen at the dawn
Descry a land far off and know not which.
So I approach uncertain; so I cruise
Round thy mysterious islet, and behold
Surf and great mountains and loud river-bars,
And from the shore hear inland voices call.
Strange is the seaman's heart; he hopes, he fears;
Draws closer and sweeps wider from that coast;
Last, his rent sail refits, and to the deep
His shattered prow uncomforted puts back.
Yet as he goes he ponders at the helm
Of that bright island; where he feared to touch,
His spirit re-adventures; and for years,
Where by his wife he slumbers safe at home,
Thoughts of that land revisit him; he sees
The eternal mountains beckon, and awakes
Yearning for that far home that might have been.

XI

TO WILL H. LOW

YOUTH now flees on feathered foot
Faint and fainter sounds the flute,
Rarer songs of gods; and still
Somewhere on the sunny hill,
Or along the winding stream,
Through the willows, flits a dream;
Flits, but shows a smiling face,
Flees, but with so quaint a grace,
None can choose to stay at home,
All must follow, all must roam.
This is unborn beauty: she
Now in air floats high and free,
Takes the sun and breaks the blue;—
Late with stooping pinion flew
Raking hedgerow trees, and wet
Her wing in silver streams, and set
Shining foot on temple roof:
Now again she flies aloof,
Coasting mountain clouds and kiss't
By the evening's amethyst.

In wet wood and miry lane,
Still we pant and pound in vain;
Still with leaden foot we chase
Waning pinion, fainting face;
Still with gray hair we stumble on,
Till, behold, the vision gone!

Where hath fleeting beauty led?
To the doorway of the dead.
Life is over, life was gay:
We have come the primrose way.

XII

TO MRS. WILL H. LOW

EVEN in the bluest noonday of July,
There could not run the smallest breath of wind
But all the quarter sounded like a wood;
And in the checkered silence and above
The hum of city cabs that sought the Bois,
Suburban ashes shivered into song.
A patter and a chatter and a chirp
And a long-dying hiss—it was as though
Starched old brocaded dames through all the house
Had trailed a strident skirt, or the whole sky
Even in a wink had over-brimmed in rain.
Hark, in these shady parlors, how it talks
Of the near autumn, how the smitten ash
Trembles and augurs floods! O not too long
In these inconstant latitudes delay,
O not too late from the unbeloved north
Trim your escape! For soon shall this low roof
Resound indeed with rain, soon shall your eyes
Search the foul garden, search the darkened rooms;
Nor find one jewel but the blazing log.

12 *Rue Vernier, Paris.*

XIII

TO H. F. BROWN

(*Written During a Dangerous Sickness*)

I SIT and wait a pair of oars
On cis-Elysian river-shores.
Where the immortal dead have sate,
'Tis mine to sit and meditate;
To re-ascend life's rivulet,
Without remorse, without regret;
And sing my *Alma Genetrix*
Among the willows of the Styx.

And lo, as my serener soul
Did these unhappy shores patrol,
And wait with an attentive ear
The coming of the gondolier,
Your fire-surviving roll I took,
Your spirited and happy book;*
Whereon, despite my frowning fate,
It did my soul so recreate
That all my fancies fled away
On a Venetian holiday.

Now, thanks to your triumphant care,
Your pages clear as April air,
The sails, the bells, the birds, I know,
And the far-off Friulan snow;

* "Life on the Lagoons," by H. F. Brown, originally burned
in the fire at Messrs. Kegan Paul, Trench & Co.'s.

The land and sea, the sun and shade,
And the blue even lamp-inlaid,
For this, for these, for all, O friend,
For your whole book from end to end—
For Paron Piero's muttonham—
I your defaulting debtor am.

Perchance, reviving, yet may I
To your sea-paven city hie,
And in a *felze,* some day yet
Light at your pipe my cigarette.

XIV

TO ANDREW LANG

DEAR Andrew, with the brindled hair,
Who glory to have thrown in air
High over arm, the trembling reed,
By Ale and Kail, by Till and Tweed;
An equal craft of hand you show
The pen to guide, the fly to throw;
I count you happy starred; for God,
When He with inkpot and with rod
Endowed you, bade your fortune lead
Forever by the crooks of Tweed,
Forever by the woods of song
And lands that to the Muse belong;
Or if in peopled streets, or in
The abhorred pedantic sanhedrim,
It should be yours to wander, still
Airs of the morn, airs of the hill,

The plovery Forest and the seas
That break about the Hebrides,
Should follow over field and plain
And find you at the window-pane;
And you again see hill and peel,
And the bright springs gush at your heel.
So went the fiat forth, and so
Garrulous like a brook you go,
With sound of happy mirth and sheen
Of daylight—whether by the green
You fare that moment, or the gray;
Whether you dwell in March or May;
Or whether treat of reels and rods
Or of the old unhappy gods:
Still like a brook your page has shone,
And your ink sings of Helicon.

XV

ET TU IN ARCADIA VIXISTI

(*To R. A. M. S.*)

IN ancient tales, O friend, thy spirit dwelt;
There, from of old, thy childhood passed; and there
High expectation, high delights and deeds,
Thy fluttering heart with hope and terror moved.
And thou hast heard of yore the Blatant Beast,
And Roland's horn, and that war-scattering shout
Of all-unarmed Achilles, ægis-crowned.
And perilous lands thou sawest, sounding shores

And seas and forests drear, island and dale
And mountain dark. For thou with Tristram rod'st
Or Bedevere, in farthest Lyonesse
Thou hadst a booth in Samarcand, whereat
Side-looking Magians trafficked; thence, by night,
An Afreet snatched thee, and with wings upbore
Beyond the Aral mount; or hoping gain,
Thou, with a jar of money didst embark
For Balsorah, by sea. But chiefly thou
In that clear air took'st life; in Arcady
The haunted, land of song; and by the wells
Where most the gods frequent. There Chiron old,
In the Pelethronian antre, taught thee lore:
The plants, he taught, and by the shining stars
In forests dim to steer. There hast thou seen
Immortal Pan dance secret in a glade,
And, dancing, roll his eyes; these where they fell,
Shed glee, and through the congregated oaks
A flying horror winged; while all the earth
To the god's pregnant footing thrilled within.
Or whiles, beside the sobbing stream, he breathed,
In his clutched pipe unformed and wizard strains
Divine yet brutal; which the forest heard,
And thou, with awe; and far upon the plain
The unthinking plowman started and gave ear.
Now things there are that, upon him who sees,
A strong vocation lay; and strains there are
That whoso hears shall hear for evermore.
For evermore thou hear'st a mortal Pan
And those melodious godheads, ever young
And ever quiring on the mountains old.

What was this earth, child of the gods, to thee?
Forth from thy dreamland thou, a dreamer cam'st
And in thine ears the olden music rang,
And in thy mind the doings of the dead,
And those heroic ages long forgot.
To a so fallen earth, alas! too late,
Alas! in evil days, thy steps return,
To list at noon for nightingales, to grow
A dweller on the beach till Argo come
That came long since, a lingerer by the pool
Where that desired angel bathes no more.

As when the Indian to Dakota comes
Or farthest Idaho, and where he dwelt,
He with his clan, a humming city finds;
Thereon a while, amazed, he stares, and then
To right and leftward, like a questing dog,
Seeks first the ancestral altars, then the hearth
Long cold with rains, and where old terror lodged,
And where the dead. So thee undying Hope,
With all her pack, hunts screaming through the
        years:
Here, there, thou fleest; but nor here nor there
The pleasant gods abide, the glory dwells.

That, that was not Apollo, not the god.
This was not Venus, though she Venus seemed
A moment. And though fair yon river move,
She, all the way from disenchanted fount
To seas unhallowed runs; the gods forsook
Long since her trembling rushes; from her plains

Disconsolate, long since adventure fled;
And now although the inviting river flows
And every poplared cape and every bend
Or willowy islet, win upon thy soul
And to thy hopeful shallop whisper speed;
Yet hope not thou at all; hope is no more;
And O, long since the golden groves are dead
The faery cities vanished from the land!

XVI

TO W. E. HENLEY

THE years runs through her phases; rain and sun,
Springtime and summer pass; winter succeeds;
But one pale season rules the house of death.
Cold falls the imprisoned daylight; fell disease
By each lean pallet squats, and pain and sleep
Toss gaping on the pillows.

                        But O thou!
Uprise and take thy pipe. Bid music flow,
Strains by good thoughts attended, like the spring
The swallows follow over land and sea.
Pain sleeps at once; at once, with open eyes,
Dozing despair awakes. The shepherd sees
His flock come bleating home; the seaman hears
Once more the cordage rattle. Airs of home!
Youth, love and roses blossom; the gaunt ward
Dislimns and disappears, and, opening out,
Shows brooks and forests, and the blue beyond
Of mountains.

Small the pipe; but oh! do thou,
Peak-faced and suffering piper, blow therein
The dirge of heroes dead; and to these sick,
These dying, sound the triumph over death.
Behold! each greatly breathes; each tastes a joy
Unknown before, in dying; for each knows
A hero dies with him—though unfulfilled,
Yet conquering truly—and not dies in vain.

So is pain cheered, death comforted; the house
Of sorrow smiles to listen.   Once again—
O thou, Orpheus and Heracles, the bard
And the deliverer, touch the stops again!

XVII

HENRY JAMES

WHO comes to-night?   We ope the doors in vain.
Who comes?   My bursting walls, can you contain
The presences that now together throng
Your narrow entry, as with flowers and song,
As with the air of life, the breath of talk?
Lo, how these fair immaculate women walk
Behind their jocund maker; and we see
Slighted *De Mauves,* and that far different she,
Gressie, the trivial sphynx; and to our feast
Daisy and *Barb* and *Chancellor* (she not least!)
With all their silken, all their airy kin,
Do like unbidden angels enter in.
But he, attended by these shining names,
Comes (best of all) himself—our welcome James.

XVIII

THE MIRROR SPEAKS

WHERE the bells peal far at sea
Cunning fingers fashioned me.
There on palace walls I hung
While that Consuelo sung;
But I heard, though I listened well,
Never a note, never a trill,
Never a beat of the chiming bell.
There I hung and looked, and there
In my gray face, faces fair
Shone from under shining hair.
Well I saw the poising head,
But the lips moved and nothing said;
And when lights were in the hall,
Silent moved the dancers all.

So a while I glowed, and then
Fell on dusty days and men;
Long I slumbered packed in straw,
Long I none but dealers saw;
Till before my silent eye
One that sees came passing by.

Now with an outlandish grace,
To the sparkling fire I face
In the blue room at Skerryvore;
Where I wait until the door
Open, and the Prince of Men,
Henry James, shall come again.

XIX

KATHARINE

WE see you as we see a face
That trembles in a forest place
Upon the mirror of a pool
Forever quiet, clear and cool;
And in the wayward glass appears
To hover between smiles and tears
Elfin and human, airy and true,
And backed by the reflected blue.

XX

TO F. J. S.

I READ, dear friend, in your dear face
Your life's tale told with perfect grace;
The river of your life I trace
Up the sun-checkered, devious bed
To the far-distant fountain-head.
Not one quick beat of your warm heart,
Nor thought that came to you apart,
Pleasure nor pity, love nor pain
Nor sorrow, has gone by in vain;
But as some lone, wood-wandering child
Brings home with him at evening mild
The thorns and flowers of all the wild,
From your whole life, O fair and true,
Your flowers and thorns you bring with you!

XXI

REQUIEM

UNDER the wide and starry sky,
Dig the grave and let me lie.
Glad did I live and gladly die,
   And I laid me down with a will.

This be the verse you grave for me:
Here he lies where he longed to be;
Home is the sailor, home from sea,
   And the hunter home from the hill.

XXII

THE CELESTIAL SURGEON

IF I have faltered more or less
In my great task of happiness;
If I have moved among my race
And shown no glorious morning face;
If beams from happy human eyes
Have moved me not; if morning skies,
Books, and my food, and summer rain
Knocked on my sullen heart in vain:—
Lord, thy most pointed pleasure take
And stab my spirit broad awake;
Or, Lord, if too obdurate I,
Choose thou, before that spirit die,
A piercing pain, a killing sin,
And to my dead heart run them in!

XXIII

OUR LADY OF THE SNOWS

OUT of the sun, out of the blast,
Out of the world, alone I passed
Across the moor and through the wood
To where the monastery stood.
There neither lute nor breathing fife,
Nor rumor of the world of life,
Nor confidences low and dear,
Shall strike the meditative ear.
Aloof, unhelpful, and unkind,
The prisoners of the iron mind,
Where nothing speaks except the hell
The unfraternal brothers dwell.

Poor, passionate men, still clothed afresh
With agonizing folds of flesh;
Whom the clear eyes solicit still
To some bold output of the will,
While fairy Fancy far before
And musing Memory-Hold-the-door
Now to heroic death invite
And now uncurtain fresh delight:
O, little boots it thus to dwell
On the remote unneighbored hill!

O, to be up and doing, O
Unfearing and unshamed to go
In all the uproar and the press

About my human business!
My undissuaded heart I hear
Whisper courage in my ear.
With voiceless calls, the ancient earth
Summons me to a daily birth.
Thou, O my love, ye, O my friends—
The gist of life, the end of ends—
To laugh, to love, to live, to die,
Ye call me by the ear and eye!

Forth from the casemate, on the plain
Where honor has the world to gain,
Pour forth and bravely do your part,
O knights of the unshielded heart!
Forth and forever forward!—out
From prudent turret and redoubt,
And in the mellay charge amain,
To fall, but yet to rise again!
Captive? ah, still, to honor bright,
A captive soldier of the right!
Or free and fighting, good with ill?
Unconquering but unconquered still!

And ye, O brethren, what if God,
When from heav'n's top he spies abroad,
And sees on this tormented stage
The noble war of mankind rage:
What if his vivifying eye,
O monks, should pass your corner by?
For still the Lord is Lord of might;
In deeds, in deeds, he takes delight;

The plow, the spear, the laden barks,
The field, the founded city, marks;
He marks the smiler of the streets,
The singer upon garden seats;
He sees the climber in the rocks:
To him the shepherd folds his flocks.
For those he loves that underprop
With daily virtues heaven's top,
And bearing the falling sky with ease,
Unfrowning caryatides.

Those he approves that ply the trade,
That rock the child, that wed the maid,
That with weak virtues, weaker hands,
Sow gladness on the peopled lands,
And still with laughter, song and shout,
Spin the great wheel of earth about.

But ye?—O ye who linger still,
Here in your fortress on the hill,
With placid face, with tranquil breath,
The unsought volunteers of death,
Our cheerful General on high
With careless looks may pass you by.

XXIV

NOT yet, my soul, these friendly fields desert,
Where thou with grass, and rivers, and the breeze,
And the bright face of day, thy dalliance hadst;
Where to thine ear first sang the enraptured birds;

Where love and thou lasting bargain made.
The ship rides trimmed, and from the eternal shore
Thou hearest airy voices; but not yet
Depart, my soul, not yet a while depart.

Freedom is far, rest far.   Thou art with life
Too closely woven, nerve with nerve entwined;
Service still craving service, love for love,
Love for dear love, still suppliant with tears.
Alas, not yet thy human task is done!
A bond at birth is forged; a debt doth lie
Immortal on mortality.   It grows—
By vast rebound it grows, unceasing growth;
Gift upon gift, alms upon alms, upreared,
From man, from God, from nature, till the soul
At that so huge indulgence stands amazed.

Leave not, my soul, the unfoughten field, nor leave
Thy debts dishonored, nor thy place desert
Without due service rendered.   For thy life,
Up, spirit, and defend that fort of clay,
Thy body, now beleaguered; whether soon
Or late she fall; whether to-day thy friends
Bewail thee dead, or, after years, a man
Grown old in honor and the friend of peace.
Contend, my soul, for moments and for hours;
Each is with service pregnant; each reclaimed
Is as a kingdom conquered, where to reign.
As when a captain rallies to the fight
His scattered legions, and beats ruin back,
He, on the field, encamps, well pleased in mind.
Yet surely him shall fortune overtake,

Him smite in turn, headlong his ensigns drive;
And that dear land, now safe, to-morrow fall.
But he, unthinking, in the present good
Solely delights, and all the camps rejoice.

XXV

IT is not yours, O mother, to complain,
Not, mother, yours to weep,
Though nevermore your son again
Shall to your bosom creep,
Though nevermore again you watch
      your baby sleep.

Though in the greener paths of earth,
Mother and child no more
We wander; and no more the birth
Of me whom once you bore
Seems still the brave reward that
      once it seemed of yore;

Though as all passes, day and night,
The seasons and the years,
From you, O mother, this delight,
This also disappears—
Some profit yet survives of all your
      pangs and tears.

The child, the seed, the grain of corn,
The acorn on the hill,

Each for some separate end is born
In season fit, and still
Each must in strength arise to work
      the almighty will.

So from the hearth the children flee,
By that almighty hand
Austerly led; so one by sea
Goes forth, and one by land;
Nor aught of all man's sons escape from
      that command.

So from the sally each obeys
The unseen almighty nod;
So till the ending all their ways
Blindfolded loth have trod:
Nor knew their task at all, but were the
      tools of God.

And as the fervent smith of yore
Beat out the glowing blade,
Nor wielded in the front of war
The weapons that he made,
But in the tower at home still plied his
      ringing trade;

So like a sword the son shall roam
On nobler missions sent;
And as the smith remained at home
In peaceful turret pent,
So sits the while at home the mother
      well content.

XXVI

THE SICK CHILD

Child

    O MOTHER, lay your hand on my brow!
    O mother, mother, where am I now?
    Why is the room so gaunt and great?
    Why am I lying awake so late?

Mother

    Fear not at all: the night is still;
    Nothing is here that means you ill—
    Nothing but lamps the whole town through,
    And never a child awake but you.

Child

    Mother, mother, speak low in my ear,
    Some of the things are so great and near,
    Some are so small and far away,
    I have a fear that I cannot say.
    What have I done, and what do I fear,
    And why are you crying, mother dear?

Mother

    Out in the city, sounds begin,
    Thank the kind God, the carts come in!
    An hour or two more, and God is so kind,
    The day shall be blue in the window-blind,
    Then shall my child go sweetly asleep,
    And dream of the birds and the hills of sheep.

XXVII

IN MEMORIAM F. A. S.

YET, O stricken heart, remember, O remember
    How of human days he lived the better part.
April came to bloom and never dim December
    Breathed its killing chills upon the head or heart.

Doomed to know not Winter, only Spring, a being
    Trod the flowery April blithely for a while,
Took his fill of music, joy of thought and seeing,
    Came and stayed and went, nor ever ceased to
      smile.

Came and stayed and went, and now when all is
      finished,
    You alone have crossed the melancholy stream,
Yours the pang, but his, O his, the undiminished
    Undecaying gladness, undeparted dream.

All that life contains of torture, toil, and treason,
    Shame, dishonor, death, to him were but a name.
Here, a boy, he dwelt through all the singing season
    And ere the day of sorrow departed as he came.

Davos, 1881.

XXVIII

TO MY FATHER

PEACE and her huge invasion to these shores
Puts daily home; innumerable sails
Dawn on the far horizon and draw near;
Innumerable loves, uncounted hopes
To our wild coasts, not darkling now, approach:
Not now obscure, since thou and thine are there,
And bright on the lone isle, the foundered reef,
The long, resounding foreland, Pharos stands.

These are thy works, O father, these thy crown;
Whether on high the air be pure, they shine
Along the yellowing sunset, and all night
Among the unnumbered stars of God they shine;
Or whether fogs arise and far and wide
The low sea-level drown—each finds a tongue
And all night long the tolling bell resounds:
So shine, so toll, till night be overpast,
Till the stars vanish, till the sun return,
And in the haven rides the fleet secure.

In the first hour, the seaman in his skiff
Moves through the unmoving bay, to where the town
Its earliest smoke into the air upbreathes
And the rough hazels climb along the beach.
To the tugg'd oar the distant echo speaks.
The ship lies resting, where by reef and roost
Thou and thy lights have led her like a child.

This hast thou done, and I—can I be base?
I must arise, O father, and to port
Some lost, complaining seaman pilot home.

XXIX

IN THE STATES

WITH half a heart I wander here
　　As from an age gone by
A brother—yet though young in years,
　　An elder brother, I.

You speak another tongue than mine,
　　Though both were English born.
I toward the night of time decline,
　　You mount into the morn.

Youth shall grow great and strong and free,
　　But age must still decay:
To-morrow for the States—for me,
　　England and Yesterday.

San Francisco.

XXX

A PORTRAIT

I AM a kind of farthing dip,
　　Unfriendly to the nose and eyes;
A blue-behinded ape, I skip
　　Upon the trees of Paradise.

At mankind's feast, I take my place
   In solemn, sanctimonious state,
And have the air of saying grace
   While I defile the dinner-plate.

I am "the smiler with the knife,"
   The battener upon garbage, I—
Dear Heaven, with such a rancid life,
   Were it not better far to die?

Yet still, about the human pale,
   I love to scamper, love to race,
To swing by my irreverent tail
   All over the most holy place;

And when at length, some golden day,
   The unfailing sportsman, aiming at,
Shall bag, me—all the world shall say,
   Thank God, and there's an end of that!

XXXI

SING clearlier, Muse, or evermore be still,
Sing truer or no longer sing!
No more the voice of melancholy Jacques
To wake a weeping echo in the hill;
But as the boy, the pirate of the spring,
From the green elm a living linnet takes,
One natural verse recapture—then be still.

XXXII

A CAMP *

THE bed was made, the room was fit
By punctual eve the stars were lit;
The air was still, the water ran,
No need was there for maid or man,
When we put up, my ass and I,
At God's green caravanserai.

XXXIII

THE COUNTRY OF THE CAMISARDS †

WE traveled in the print of olden wars,
    Yet all the land was green
    And love we found, and peace,
    Where fire and war had been.

They pass and smile, the children of the sword—
    No more the sword they wield;
    And O, how deep the corn
    Along the battlefield!

XXXIV

SKERRYVORE

FOR love of lovely words and for the sake
Of those, my kinsmen and my countrymen,
Who early and late in the windy ocean toiled

* From "Travels with a Donkey."   † Ibid.

To plant a star for seamen, where was then
The surfy haunt of seals and cormorants:
I, on the lintel of this cot, inscribe
The name of a strong tower.

XXXV

SKERRYVORE: *THE PARALLEL*

HERE all is sunny, and when the truant gull
Skims the green level of the lawn, his wing
Dispetals roses; here the house is framed
Of kneaded brick and the plumed mountain pine,
Such clay as artists fashion and such wood
As the tree-climbing urchin breaks. But there
Eternal granite hewn from the living isle
And dowelled with brute iron, rears a tower
That from its wet foundation to its crown
Of glittering glass, stands, in the sweep of winds,
Immovable, immortal, eminent.

XXXVI

MY house, I say. But hark to the sunny doves
That make my roof the arena of their loves,
That gyre about the gable all day long
And fill the chimneys with their murmurous song:
Our house, they say; and *mine,* the cat declares
And spreads his golden fleece upon the chairs;
And *mine,* the dog, and rises stiff with wrath
If any alien foot profane the path.

So too the buck that trimmed my terraces,
Our whilome gardener, called the garden his;
Who now, deposed, surveys my plain abode
And his late kingdom, only from the road.

XXXVII

MY body which my dungeon is,
And yet my parks and palaces:—
   Which is so great that there I go
All the day long to and fro,
And when the night begins to fall
Throw down my bed and sleep, while all
The building hums with wakefulness—
Even as a child of savages
When evening takes her on her way,
(She having roamed a summer's day
Along the mountain-sides and scalp)
Sleeps in an antre of that alp:—
   Which is so broad and high that there,
As in the topless fields of air,
My fancy soars like to a kite
And faints in the blue infinite:—
   Which is so strong, my strongest throes
And the rough world's besieging blows
Not break it, and so weak withal,
Death ebbs and flows in its loose wall
As the green sea in fishers' nets,
And tops its topmost parapets:—
   Which is so wholly mine that I

Can wield its whole artillery,
And mine so little, that my soul
Dwells in perpetual control,
And I but think and speak and do
As my dead fathers move me to:—
　　If this born body of my bones
The beggared soul so barely owns,
What money passed from hand to hand,
What creeping custom of the land,
What deed of author or assign,
Can make a house a thing of mine?

XXXVIII

SAY not of me that weakly I declined
The labors of my sires, and fled the sea,
The towers we founded and the lamps we lit,
To play at home with paper like a child.
But rather say: *In the afternoon of time
A strenuous family dusted from its hands
The sand of granite, and beholding far
Along the sounding coast its pyramids
And tall memorials catch the dying sun,
Smiled well content, and to this childish task
Around the fire addressed its evening hours.*

TABLE OF COMMON SCOTTISH VOWEL SOUNDS

ae
ai } = open A as in rare.

a'
au } = AW as in law.
aw

ea = open E as in mere, but this with exceptions, as heather = heather, wean = wain, lear = liar.

ee
ei } = open E as in mere.
ie

oa = open O as in more.

ou = doubled O as in poor.

ow = OW as in Bower.

u = doubled O as in poor.

ui or ü before R = (say roughly) open A as in rare.

ui or ü before any other consonant = (say roughly) close I as in grin.

y = open I as in kite.

i = pretty nearly what you please, much as in English. Heaven guide the reader through that labyrinth! But in Scots it dodges usually from the short I, as in grin, to the open E, as in mere. Find and blind, I may remark, are pronounced to rhyme with the preterite of grin.

BOOK II: IN SCOTS

I

THE MAKER TO POSTERITY

FAR 'yont amang the years to be
When a' we think, an' a' we see,
An' a' we luve, 's been dung ajee
    By time's rouch shouther,
An' what was richt and wrang for me
    Lies mangled throu'ther,

It's possible—it's hardly mair—
That some ane, ripin' after lear—
Some auld professor or young heir,
    If still there's either—
May find an' read me, an' be sair
    Perplexed, puir brither!

"What tongue does your auld bookie speak?"
He'll spier; an' I, his mou to steik:
"No bein' fit to write in Greek,
    I wrote in Lallan,
Dear to my heart as the peat reek,
    Auld as Tantallon.

"Few spak it than, an' noo there's nane.
My puir auld sangs lie a' their lane,

Their sense, that aince was braw an' plain,
    Tint a'thegether,
Like runes upon a standin' stane
    Amang the heather.

"But think not you the brae to speel;
You, tae, maun chow the bitter peel;
For a' your lear, for a' your skeel,
    Ye're nane sae lucky;
An' things are mebbe waur than weel
    For you, my buckie.

"The hale concern (baith hens an eggs,
Baith books an' writers, stars an' clegs)
Noo stachers upon lowsent legs
    An' wears awa';
The tack o' mankind, near the dregs,
    Rins unco law.

"Your book, that in some braw new tongue,
Ye wrote or prentit, preached or sung,
Will still be just a bairn, an' young
    In fame an' years,
Whan the hale planet's guts are dung
    About your ears;

"An' you, sair gruppin' to a spar
Or whammled wi' some bleezin' star,
Cryin' to ken whaur deil ye are,
    Hame, France, or Flanders—
Whang sindry like a railway car
    An' flie in danders."

II

ILLE TERRARUM

FRAE nirly, nippin', Eas'lan' breeze,
Frae Norlan' snaw, an' haar o' seas,
Weel happit in your garden trees,
        A bonny bit,
Atween the muckle Pentland's knees,
        Secure ye sit.

Beeches an' aiks entwine their theek,
An' firs, a stench, auld-farrant clique.
A' simmer day, your chimleys reek,
        Couthy and bien;
An' here an' there your windies keek
        Amang the green.

A pickle plats an' paths an' posies,
A wheen auld gillyflowers an' roses:
A ring o' wa's the hale incloses
        Frae sheep or men;
An' there the auld housie beeks and dozes
        A' by her lane.

The gairdner crooks his weary back
A' day in the pitaty-track,
Or maybe stops a while to crack
        Wi' Jane the cook,
Or at some buss, worm-eaten-black,
        To gie a look.

Frae the high hills the curlew ca's;
The sheep gang baaing by the wa's;
Or whiles a clan o' roosty craws
　　　　Cangle together;
The wild bees seek the gairden raws,
　　　　Weariet wi' heather.

Or in the gloamin' douce an' gray
The sweet-throat mavis tunes her lay;
The herd comes linkin' doun the brae;
　　　　An' by degrees
The muckle siller müne maks way
　　　　Amang the trees.

Here aft hae I, wi' sober heart,
For meditation sat apairt,
When orra loves or kittle art
　　　　Perplexed my mind;
Here socht a balm for ilka smart
　　　　O' humankind.

Here aft, weel neukit by my lane,
Wi' Horace, or perhaps Montaigne,
The mornin' hours hae come an' gane
　　　　Abüne my heid—
I wadnae gi'en a chucky-stane
　　　　For a' I'd read.

But noo the auld city, street by street,
An' winter fu' o' snaw an' sleet,
A while shut in my gangrel feet
　　　　An' goavin' mettle;

Noo is the soopit ingle sweet,
    An' liltin' kettle.

An' noo the winter winds complain;
Cauld lies the glaur in ilka lane;
On draigled hizzie, tautit wean
    An' drucken lads,
In the mirk nicht, the winter rain
    Dribbles an' blads.

Whan bugles frae the Castle rock,
An' beaten drums wi' dowie shock,
Wauken, at cauld-rife sax o'clock,
    My chitterin' frame,
I mind me on the kintry cock,
    The kintry hame.

I mind me on yon bonny bield;
An' Fancy traivels far afield
To gaither a' that gairdens yield
    O' sun an' Simmer:
To hearten up a dowie chield,
    Fancy's the limmer!

III

WHEN aince Aprile has fairly come,
An' birds may bigg in winter's lum,
An' pleisure's spreid for a' and some
An' pleisure's spread for a' and some
    O' whatna state,
Love, wi' her auld recruitin' drum,
    Than taks the gate.

The heart plays dunt wi' main an' micht;
The lasses' een are a' sae bricht,
Their dresses are sae braw an' ticht,
　　　The bonny birdies!—
Puir winter virtue at the sicht
　　　Gangs heels ower hurdies.

An' aye as love frae land to land
Tirls the drum wi' eident hand,
A' men collect at her command,
　　　Toun-bred or land'art,
An' follow in a denty band
　　　Her gaucy standart.

An' I, wha sang o' rain an' snaw,
An' weary winter weel awa',
Noo busk me in a jacket braw,
　　　An' tak my place
I' the ram-stam, harum-scarum raw,
　　　Wi' smilin' face.

IV

A MILE AN' A BITTOCK

A MILE an' a bittock, a mile or twa,
Abüne the burn, ayont the law,
Davie an' Donal' an' Cherlie an' a',
　　　An' the müne was shinin' clearly!

Ane went hame wi' the ither, an' then
The ither went hame wi' the ither twa men,
An' baith wad return him the service again,
 An' the müne was shinin' clearly!

The clocks were chappin' in house an' ha',
Eleeven, twal an' ane an' twa;
An' the guidman's face was turnt to the wa',
 An' the müne was shinin' clearly!

A wind got up frae affa the sea,
It blew the stars as clear's could be,
It blew in the een of a' o' the three,
 An' the müne was shinin' clearly!

Noo, Davie was first to get sleep in his head,
"The best o' frien's maun twine," he said;
"I'm weariet, an' here I'm awa' to my bed."
 An' the müne was shinin' clearly!

Twa o' them walkin' an' crackin' in their lane,
The mornin' licht cam gray an' plain,
An' the birds they yammert on stick an' stane,
 An' the müne was shinin' clearly!

O years ayont, O years awa',
My lads, ye'll mind whate'er befa'—
My lads, ye'll mind on the bield o' the law,
 When the müne was shinin' clearly.

V

A LOWDEN SABBATH MORN

THE clinkum-clark o' Sabbath bells
Noo to the hoastin' rookery swells,
Noo faintin' laigh in shady dells,
    Sounds far an' near,
An' through the simmer kintry tells
    Its tale o' cheer.

An' noo, to that melodious play,
A' deidly awn the quiet sway—
A' ken their solemn holiday,
    Bestial an' human,
The singin' lintie on the brae,
    The restin' plou'man.

He, mair than a' the lave o' men,
His week completit joys to ken;
Half-dressed, he daunders out an' in,
    Perplext wi' leisure;
An' his raxt limbs he'll rax again
    Wi' painfü' pleesure.

The steerin' mither strang afit
Noo shoos the bairnies but a bit;
Noo cries them ben, their Sinday Shüit
    To scart upon them,
Or sweeties in their pouch to pit,
    Wi' blessin's on them.

The lasses, clean frae tap to taes,
Are busked in crunklin' underclaes;
The gartened hose, the weel-filled stays,
    The nakit shift,
A' bleached on bonny greens for days,
    An' white's the drift.

An' noo to face the kirkward mile:
The guidman's hat o' dacent style,
The blackit shoon, we noo maun fyle
    As white's the miller;
A waefü' peety tae, to spile
    The warth o' siller.

Our Marg'et, aye sae keen to crack,
Douce-stappin' in the stoury track,
Her emeralt goun a' kiltit back
    Frae snawy coats,
White-ankled, leads the kirkward pack
    Wi' Dauvit Groats.

A thocht ahint, in runkled breeks
A' spiled wi' lyin' by for weeks,
The guidman follows closs, an' cleiks
    The sonsie missis;
His sarious face at aince bespeaks
    The day that this is.

And aye an' while we nearer draw
To whaur the kirton lies alaw,
Mair neebors, comin' saft an' slaw
    Frae here an' there,

The thicker thrang the gate an' caw
    The stour in air.

But hark! the bells frae nearer clang;
To rowst the slaw, their sides they bang;
An' see! black coats a'ready thrang
    The green kirkyaird,
And at the yett, the chestnuts spang
    That brocht the laird.

The solemn elders at the plate
Stand drinkin' deep the pride o' state:
That practiced hands as gash an' great
    As Lords o' Session;
The later named, a wee thing blate
    In their expression.

The prentit stanes that mark the deid,
Wi' lengthened lip, the sarious read;
Syne wag a moraleesin' heid,
    An' then an' there
Their hirplin' practice an' their creed
    Try hard to square.

It's here our Merren lang has lain,
A wee bewast the table-stane;
An' yon's the grave o' Sandy Blane;
    An' further ower,
The mither's brithers, dacent men!
    Lie a' the fower.

Here the guidman sall bide awee
To dwall amang the deid; to see
Auld faces clear in fancy's e'e;
    Belike to hear
Auld voices fa'in' saft an' slee
    On fancy's ear.

Thus, on the day o' solemn things,
The bell that in the steeple swings
To fauld a scaittered faim'ly rings
    Its walcome screed;
An' just a wee thing nearer brings
    The quick an' deid.

But noo the bell is ringin' in;
To tak their places, folk begin;
The minister himsel' will shüne
    Be up the gate,
Filled fu' wi' clavers about sin
    An' man's estate.

The tünes are up—*French,* to be shüre,
The faithfü' *French,* an' twa-three mair.
The auld prezentor, hoastin' sair,
    Wales out the portions,
An' yirks the tüne into the air
    Wi' queer contortions.

Follows the prayer, the readin' next,
An' than the fisslin' for the text—

The twa-three last to find it, vext
     But kind o' proud;
An' than the peppermints are raxed,
     An' southernwood.

For noo's the time whan pows are seen
Nid-noddin' like a mandareen;
When tenty mithers stap a preen
     In sleepin' weans;
An' nearly half the parochine
     Forget their pains.

There's just a waukrif' twa or three:
Thrawn commentautors sweer to 'gree,
Weans glowrin' at the bumblin' bee
     On the windie-glasses,
Or lads that tak a keek a-glee.
     At sonsie lasses.

Himsel', meanwhile, frae whaur he cocks
An' bobs belaw the soundin'-box,
The treesures of his words unlocks
     Wi' prodigality,
An' deals some unco dingin' knocks
     To infidality.

Wi' sappy unction, hoo he burkes
The hopes o' men that trust in works,
Expounds the fau'ts o' ither kirks,
     An' shaws the best o' them
No muckle better than mere Turks,
     When a's confessed o' them.

Bethankit! what a bonny creed!
What mair would ony Christian need?—
The braw words rumm'le ower his heid,
  Nor steer the sleeper;
An' in their restin' graves, the deid
  Sleep aye the deeper.

Note.—It may be guessed by some that I had a certain parish in my eye, and this makes it proper I should add a word of disclamation. In my time there have been two ministers in that parish. Of the first I have a special reason to speak well, even had there been any to think ill. The second I have often met in private and long (in the due phrase) "sat under" in his church, and neither here nor there have I heard an unkind or ugly word upon his lips. The preacher of the text had thus no original in that particular parish; but when I was a boy, he might have been observed in many others; he was then (like the schoolmaster) abroad; and by recent advices, it would seem he has not yet entirely disappeared.

VI

THE SPAEWIFE

O, I wad like to ken—to the beggar-wife says I—
Why chops are guid to brander and nane sae good
  to fry.
An' siller, that's sae braw to keep, is brawer still
  to gi'e.
—*It's gey an easy spierin'*, says the beggar-wife
  to me.

O, I wad like to ken—to the beggar-wife says I—
Hoo a' things come to be whaur we find them when
  we try,

The lasses in their claes an' the fishes in the sea.
—*It's gey an easy spierin'*, says the beggar-wife
to me.

O, I wad like to ken—to the beggar-wife says I—
Why lads are a' to sell an' lasses a' to buy;
An' naebody for dacency but barely twa or three.
—*It's gey an easy spierin'*, says the beggar-wife
to me.

O, I wad like to ken—to the beggar-wife says I—
Gin death's as shüre to men as killin' is to kye,
Why God has filled the yearth sae fu' o' tasty things
to pree.
—*It's gey an easy spierin'*, says the beggar-wife
to me.

O, I wad like to ken—to the beggar-wife says I—
The reason o' the cause an' the wherefore o' the why,
Wi' mony anither riddle brings the tear into my e'e.
—*It's gey an easy spierin'*, says the beggar-wife
to me.

VII

THE BLAST—1875

IT'S rainin'. Weet's the gairden sod
Weet the lang roads whaur gangrels plod—
A maist unceevil thing o' God
        In mid July—
If ye'll just curse the sneckdraw, dod!
        An' sae wull I!

He's a braw place in heev'n, ye ken,
An' lea's us puir, forjaskit men
Clamjamfried in the but and ben
      He ca's the earth—
A wee bit inconvenient den
      No muckle worth;

An' whiles, at orra times, keeks out,
Sees what puir mankind are about;
An' if He can, I've little doubt,
      Upsets their plans;
He hates a' mankind, brainch and root,
      An' a' that's man's.

An' whiles, whan they tak heart again,
An' life i' the sun looks braw an' plain,
Doun comes a jaw o' droukin' rain
      Upon their honors—
God sends a spate outower the plain,
      Or mebbe thun'ers.

Lord safe us, life's an unco thing!
Simmer an' Winter, Yule an' Spring,
The damned, dour-heartit seasons bring
      A feck o' trouble.
I wadna try't to be a king—
      No, nor for double.

But since we're in it, willy-nilly,
We maun be watchfü, wise an' skilly

An' no mind ony ither billy,
        Lassie nor God.
But drink—that's my best counsel till 'e:
        Sae tak the nod.

VIII

THE COUNTERBLAST—1886

MY bonny man, the warld, it's true,
Was made for neither me nor you;
It's just a place to warstle through,
        As Job confessed o't;
And aye the best that we'll can do
        Is mak the best o't.

There's rowth o' wrang, I'm free to say:
The simmer brunt, the winter blae,
The face of earth a' fyled wi' clay
        An' dour wi' chuckies,
An' life a rough an' land'art play
        For country buckies.

An' food's anither name for clart;
An' beasts an' brambles bite an' scart;
An' what would WE be like, my heart!
        If bared o' claethin'?
—Aweel, I cannae mend your cart:
        It's that or naethin'.

A feck o' folk frae first to last
Have through this queer experience passed;

Twa-three, I ken, just damn an' blast
    The hale transaction;
But twa-three ithers, east an' wast,
    Fand satisfaction.

Whaur braid the briery muirs expand,
A waefü' an' a weary land,
The bumblebees, a gowden band,
    Are blithely hingin';
An' there the canty wanderer fand
    The laverock singin'.

Trout in the burn grow great as herr'n',
The simple sheep can find their fair'n';
The wind blaws clean about the cairn
    Wi' caller air;
The muircock an' the barefit bairn
    Are happy there.

Sic-like the howes o' life to some:
Green loans whaur they ne'er fash their thumb,
But mark the muckle winds that come,
    Soopin' an' cool,
Or hear the powrin' burnie drum
    In the shilfa's pool.

The evil wi' the guid they tak;
They ca' a gray thing gray, no black;
To a steigh brae, a stubborn back
    Addressin' daily;
An' up the rude, unbieldy track
    O' life, gang gayly.

What you would like's a palace ha',
Or Sinday parlor dink an' braw
Wi' a' things ordered in a raw
    By denty leddies.
Weel, than, ye cannae hae't; that's a'
    That to be said is.

An' since at life ye've taen the grue,
An' winnae blithely hirsle through,
Ye've fund the very thing to do—
    That's to drink speerit;
An' shüne we'll hear the last o' you—
    An' blithe to hear it!

The shoon ye coft, the life ye lead,
Ithers will heir when aince ye're deid;
They'll heir your tasteless bite o' breid,
    An' find it sappy;
They'll to your dulefü' house succeed,
    An' there be happy.

As whan a glum an' fractious wean
Has sat an' sullened by his lane
Till, wi' a rowstin' skelp, he's taen
    An' shoo'd to bed—
The ither bairns a' fa' to play'n',
    As gleg's a gled.

IX

THE COUNTERBLAST IRONICAL

IT'S strange that God should fash to frame
    The yearth and lift sae hie,
An' clean forget to explain the same
    To a gentleman like me.

They gusty, donered ither folk,
    Their weird they weel may dree;
But why present a pig in a poke
    To a gentleman like me?

They ither folk their parritch eat
    An' sup their sugared tea;
But the mind is no to be wyled wi' meat
    Wi' a gentleman like me.

They ither folk, they court their joes
    At gloamin' on the lea;
But they're made of a commoner clay, I suppose,
    Than a gentleman like me.

They ither folk, for richt or wrang,
    They suffer, bleed, or dee;
But a' thir things are an emp'y sang
    To a gentleman like me.

It's a different thing that I demand,
    Tho' humble as can be—
A statement fair in my Maker's hand
    To a gentleman like me:

A clear account writ fair an' broad,
　　An' a plain apologie;
Or the deevil a ceevil word to God
　　From a gentleman like me.

X

THEIR LAUREATE TO AN ACADEMY
CLASS DINNER CLUB

DEAR Thamson class, whaure'er I gang
It aye comes ower me wi' a spang:
"Lordsake! they Thamson lads—(deil hang
　　Or else Lord mend them!)—
An' that wanchancy annual sang
　　I ne'er can send them!"

Straucht, at the name a trusty tyke,
My conscience girrs ahint the dyke;
Straucht on my hinderlands I fyke
　　To find a rhyme t' ye;
Pleased—although mebbe no pleased-like—
　　To gie my time t' ye.

"Weel," an' says you, wi' heavin' breist,
"Sae far, sae guid, but what's the neist?
Yearly we gaither to the feast,
　　A' hopefu' men—
Yearly we skelloch 'Hang the beast—
　　Nae sang again!' "

My lads, an' what am I to say?
Ye shürely ken the Muse's way:
Yestreen, as gleg's a tyke—the day,
    Thrawn like a cuddy:
Her conduc', that to her's a play,
    Deith to a body.

Aft whan I sat an' made my mane,
Aft whan I labored burd-alane
Fishin' for rhymes an' findin' nane,
    Or nane were fit for ye—
Ye judged me cauld's a chucky stane—
    No car'n' a bit for ye!

But saw ye ne'er some pingein' bairn
As weak as a pitaty-par'n'—
Less üsed wi' guidin' horse-shoe airn
    Than steerin' crowdie—
Packed aff his lane, by moss an' cairn,
    To ca' the howdie.

Wae's me, for the puir callant than!
He wambles like a poke o' bran,
An' the lowse rein, as hard's he can,
    Pu's, trem'lin' handit;
Till, blaff! upon his hinderlan'
    Behauld him landit.

Sic-like—I awn the weary fac'—
Whan on my muse the gate I tak,
An' see her gleed e'e raxin' back
    To keek ahint her;—

To me the brig of heev'n gangs black
    As blackest winter.

"*Lordsake! we're aff,*" thinks I, "*but whaur?*
On what abhorred and whinny scaur,
Or whammled in what sea o' glaur,
    Will she desert me?
An' will she just disgrace? or waur—
    Will she no hurt me?"

Kittle the quaere! But at least
The day I've backed the fashious beast,
While she, wi' mony a spang an' reist,
    Flang heels ower bonnet;
An' a' triumphant—for your feast,
    Hae! there's your sonnet!

XI

EMBRO HIE KIRK

THE Lord Himsel' in former days
Waled out the proper tünes for praise
An' named the proper kind o' claes
    For folk to preach in:
Preceese and in the chief o' ways
    Important teachin'.

He ordered a' things, late and air';
He ordered folk to stand at prayer
(Although I cannae just mind where
    He gave the warnin')

An' pit pomatum on their hair
    On Sabbath mornin'.

The hale o' life by His commands
Was ordered to a body's hands;
But see! this *corpus juris* stands
    By a' forgotten;
An' God's religion in a' lands
    Is deid an' rotten.

While thus the lave o' mankind's lost
O' Scotland still God makes his boast—
Puir Scotland, on whase barren coast
    A score or twa
Auld wives wi' mutches an' a hoast
    Still keep His law.

In Scotland, a wheen canty, plain,
Douce kintry-leevin' folk retain
The Truth—or did so aince—alane
    Of a' men leevin';
An' noo just twa o' them remain—
    Just Begg an' Niven.

For noo, unfaithfü' to the Lord
Auld Scotland joins the rebel horde;
Her human hymn-books on the board
    She noo displays:
An' Embro Hie Kirk's been restored
    In popish ways.

O punctum temporis for action
To a' o' the reformin' faction,

If yet, by ony act or paction,
     Thocht, word, or sermon,
This dark an' damnable transaction
     Micht yet determine!

For see—as Doctor Begg explains—
Hoo easy 't's düne! a pickle weans,
Wha in the Hie Street gaither stanes
     By his instruction,
The uncovenantit, pentit panes
     Ding to destruction.

Up, Niven, or ower late—an' dash
Laigh in the glaur that carnal hash;
Let spires and pews wi' gran' stramash
     Thegether fa';
The rumlin' kist o' whustles smash
     In pieces sma'.

Noo choose ye out a walie hammer;
About the knottit buttress clam'er;
Alang the steep roof stoyt an' stammer,
     A gate mis-chancy;
On the aul' spire, the bells' hie cha'mer,
     Dance your bit dancie.

Ding, devel, dunt, destroy, an' ruin,
Wi' carnal stanes the square bestrewin',
Till your loud chaps frae Kyle to Fruin,
     Frae hell to heeven,
Tell the guid wark that baith are doin'—
     Baith Begg an' Niven.

XII

THE SCOTSMAN'S RETURN FROM ABROAD

(In a letter from Mr. Thomson to Mr. Johnstone)

IN mony a foreign pairt I've been,
An' mony an unco ferlie seen,
Since, Mr. Johnstone, you and I
Last walkit upon Cocklerye.
Wi' gleg, observant een, I pass't
By sea an' land, through East and Wast,
And still in ilka age an' station
Saw naething but abomination.
In thir uncovenantit lands
The gangrel Scot uplifts his hands
At lack of a' sectarian füsh'n,
An' cauld religious destitütion.
He rins, puir man, frae place to place,
Tries a' their graceless means o' grace,
Preacher on preacher, kirk on kirk—
This yin a stot an' thon a stirk—
A bletherin' clan, no warth a preen,
As bad as Smith of Aiberdeen!

At last, across the weary faem,
Frae far, outlandish pairts I came.
On ilka side o' me I fand
Fresh tokens o' my native land.
Wi' whatna joy I hailed them a'—
The hilltaps standin' raw by raw,
The public house, the Hielan' birks,

And a' the bonny U. P. kirks!
But maistly thee, the bluid o' Scots,
Frae Maidenkirk to John o' Grots,
The king o' drinks, as I conceive it,
Talisker, Isla, or Glenlivet!

For after years wi' a pockmantie
Frae Zanzibar to Alicante,
In mony a fash an' sair affliction
I gie't as my sincere conviction—
Of a' their foreign tricks an' pliskies,
I maist abominate their whiskies.
Nae doot, themsel's, they ken it weel,
An' wi' a hash o' leemon peel,
An' ice an' siccan filth, they ettle
The stawsome kind o' goo to settle;
Sic wersh apothecary's broos wi'
As Scotsmen scorn to fyle their moo's wi'.

An', man, I was a blithe hame-comer
When first I syndit out my rummer.
Ye should hae seen me then, wi' care
The less important pairts prepare;
Syne, weel contentit wi' it a',
Pour in the speerits wi' a jaw!
I didnae drink, I didnae speak—
I only snowkit up the reek.
I was sae pleased therein to paidle,
I sat an' plowtered wi' my ladle.

An' blithe was I, the morrow's morn,
To daunder through the stookit corn,

And after a' my strange mishanters,
Sit doun amang my ain dissenters.
An', man, it was a joy to me
The pu'pit an' the pews to see,
The pennies dirlin' in the plate,
The elders lookin' on the state;
An' 'mang the first, as it befell,
Wha should I see, sir, but yoursel'?

I was, and I will no deny it,
At the first gliff a hantle tryit
To see yoursel' in sic a station—
It seemed a doubtfü' dispensation.
The feelin' was a mere digression;
For shüne I understood the session,
An' mindin Aiken an' M'Neil,
I wondered they had düne sae weel.
I saw I had mysel' to blame;
For had I but remained at hame,
Aiblins—though no ava' deservin' 't—
They micht hae named your humble servant.

The kirk was filled, the door was steeked;
Up to the pu'pit ance I keeked;
I was mair pleased than I can tell—
It was the minister himsel'!
Proud, proud was I to see his face,
After sae lang awa' frae grace.
Pleased as I was, I'm no denyin'
Some maitters were not edifyin';
For first I fand—an' here was news!—
Mere hymn-books cockin' in the pews—

A humanized abomination,
Unfit for ony congregation.
Syne, while I still was on the tenter,
I scunnered at the new prezentor;
I thocht him gesterin' an' cauld—
A sair declension frae the auld.
Syne, as though a' the faith was wreckit,
The prayer was not what I'd exspeckit.
Himsel', as it appeared to me,
Was no the man he üsed to be.
But just as I was growin' vext
He waled a maist judeecious text,
An' launchin' into his prelections,
Swoopt, wi' a skirl, on a' defections.

O what a gale was on my speerit
To hear the p'ints o' doctrine clearit,
And a' the horrors o' damnation
Set furth wi' faithfü' ministration!
Nae shauchlin' testimony here—
We were a' damned, an' that was clear.
I owned, wi' gratitude an' wonder,
He was a pleisure to sit under.

XIII

LATE in the nicht in bed I lay,
The winds were at their weary play,
An' tirlin' wa's an' skirlin' wae
        Through heev'n they battered;—
On-ding o' hail, on-blaff o' spray,
        The tempest blattered.

The masoned house it dinled through;
It dung the ship, it cowped the coo';
The rankit aiks it overthrew,
    Had braved a' weathers;
The strang sea-gleds it took an' blew
    Awa' like feathers.

The thraes o' fear on a' were shed,
An' the hair rose, an' slumber fled,
An' lichts were lit an' prayers were said
    Through a' the kintry;
An' the cauld terror clum in bed
    Wi' a' an' sindry.

To hear in the pit-mirk on hie
The brangled collieshangie flie,
The warl' they thocht, wi' land an' sea,
    Itsel' wad cowpit;
An' for auld airn, the smashed debris
    By God be rowpit.

Meanwhile frae far Aldeboran,
To folks wi' talescopes in han',
O' ships that cowpit, winds that ran,
    Nae sign was seen,
But the wee warl' in sunshine span
    As bricht's a preen.

I, tae, by God's especial grace,
Dwall denty in a bieldy place,
Wi' hosened feet, wi' shaven face,
    Wi' dacent mainners:

A grand example to the race
    O' tautit sinners!

The wind may blaw, the heathen rage,
The deil may start on the rampage;—
The sick in bed, the thief in cage—
    What's a' to me?
Cosh in my house, a sober sage,
    I sit an' see.

An' whiles the bluid spangs to my bree,
To lie sae saft, to live sae free,
While better men maun do an' die
    In unco places.
"Whaur's God?" I cry, an' *"Whae is me*
    To hae sic graces?"

I mind the fecht the sailors keep,
But fire or can'le, rest or sleep,
In darkness an' the muckle deep;
    An' mind beside
The herd that on the hills o' sheep
    Has wandered wide.

I mind me on the hoastin' weans—
The penny joes on causey stanes—
The auld folk wi' the crazy banes,
    Baith auld an' puir,
That aye maun thole the winds an' rains
    An' labor sair.

An' whiles I'm kind o' pleased a blink,
An' kind o' fleyed forby, to think,
For a' my rowth o' meat an' drink
  An' waste o' crumb,
I'll mebbe have to thole wi' skink
  In Kingdom Come.

For God whan jowes the Judgment bell,
Wi' His ain Hand, His Leevin' Sel',
Sall ryve the guid (as Prophets tell)
  Frae them that had it;
And in the reamin' pat o' hell,
  The rich be scaddit.

O Lord, if this indeed be sae,
Let daw that sair an' happy day!
Again' the warl, grawn auld an' gray,
  Up wi' your aixe!
An' let the puir enjoy their play—
  I'll thole my paiks.

XIV

MY CONSCIENCE!

OF a' the ills that flesh can fear,
The loss o' frien's, the lack o' gear,
A yowlin' tyke, a glandered mear,
  A lassie's nonsense—
There's just ae thing I cannae bear,
  An' that's my conscience.

Whan day (an' a' excüse) has gane,
An' wark is düne, an' duty's plain,
An' to my chalmer a' my lane
     I creep apairt,
My conscience! hoo the yammerin' pain
      Stends to my heart!

A' day wi' various ends in view
The hairsts o' time I had to pu',
An' made a hash wad staw a soo,
     Let be a man!—
My conscience! whan my han's were fü',
      Whaur were ye than?

An' there were a' the lures o' life,
There pleesure skirlin' on the fife,
There anger, wi' the hotchin' knife
     Ground shairp in hell—
My conscience!—you that's like a wife!—
      Whaur was yoursel'?

I ken it fine: just waitin' here,
To gar the evil waur appear,
To clart the guid, confüse the clear,
     Mis-ca' the great,
My conscience! an' to raise a steer
      Whan a's ower late.

Sic-like, some tyke grawn auld and blind,
Whan thieves brok' through the gear to p'ind,

Has lain his dozened length an' grinned
    At the disaster;
An' the morn's mornin', wud's the wind,
    Yokes on his master.

XV

TO DOCTOR JOHN BROWN

(Whan the dear doctor, dear to a',
Was still amang us here belaw,
I seb my pipes his praise to blaw
    Wi' a' my speerit;
But noo, Dear Doctor, he's awa',
    An' ne'er can hear it.)

BY Lyne and Tyne, by Thames and Tees,
By a' the various river-Dee's,
In Mars and Manors 'yont the seas
    Or here at hame,
Whaure'er there's kindly folk to please,
    They ken your name.

They ken your name, they ken your tyke,
They ken the honey from your byke;
But mebbe after a' your fyke,
    (The trüth to tell)
It's just your honest Rab they like,
    An' no yoursel'.

As at the gowff, some canny play'r
Should tee a common ba' wi' care—
Should flourish and deleever fair
     His souple shintie—
An' the ba' rise into the air,
     A leevin' lintie:

Sae in the game we writers play,
There comes to some a bonny day,
When a dear ferlie shall repay
     Their years o' strife,
An' like your Rab, their things o' clay,
     Spreid wings o' life.

Ye scarce deserved it, I'm afraid—
You that had never learned the trade,
But just some idle mornin' strayed
     Into the schüle,
An' picked the fiddle up an' played
     Like Neil himsel'.

Your e'e was gleg, your fingers dink;
Ye didna fash yoursel' to think,
But wove, as fast as puss can link,
     Your denty wab:—
Ye stapped your pen into the ink,
     An' there was Rab!

Sinsyne, whaure'er your fortune lay
By dowie den, by canty brae,
Simmer an' winter, nicht an' day,
     Rab was aye wi' ye;

An' a' the folk on a' the way
      Were blithe to see ye.

O sir, the gods are kind indeed,
An' hauld ye for an honored heid,
That for a wee bit clarkit screed
      Sae weel reward ye,
An' lend—puir Rabbie bein' deid—
      His ghaist to guard ye.

For though, whaure'er yoursel' may be,
We've just to turn an' glisk a wee,
An' Rab at heel we're shüre to see
      Wi' gladsome caper:—
The bogle of a bogle, he—
      A ghaist o' paper!

And as the auld farrand hero sees
In hell a bogle Hercules,
Pit there the lesser deid to please,
      While he himsel'
Dwalls wi' the muckle gods at ease
      Far raised frae hell:

Sae the true Rabbie far has gane
On kindlier business o' his ain
Wi' aulder frien's; an' his breist-bane
      An' stumpie tailie,
He birstles at a new hearth stane
      By James and Ailie.

XVI

IT'S an owercome sooth for age an' youth
    And it brooks wi' nae denial,
That the dearest friends are the auldest friends
    And the young are just on trial.

There's a rival bauld wi' young an' auld
    And it's him that has bereft me;
For the sürest friends are the auldest friends
    And the maist o' mine hae left me.

There are kind hearts still, for friends to fill
    And fools to take and break them;
But the nearest friends are the auldest friends
    And the grave's the place to seek them.

BALLADS

THE SONG OF RAHÉRO

TO ORI A ORI

Ori, my brother in the island mode,
In every tongue and meaning much my friend,
This story of your country and your clan,
In your loved house, your too much honoured guest,
I made in English.   Take it, being done;
And let me sign it with the name you gave.

TERIITERA.

I. THE SLAYING OF TÁMATEA

IT fell in the days of old, as the men of Taiárapu tell,
A youth went forth to the fishing, and fortune favoured him well.
Támatéa his name: gullible, simple, and kind,
Comely of countenance, nimble of body, empty of mind,
His mother ruled him and loved him beyond the wont of a wife,
Serving the lad for eyes and living herself in his life.
Alone from the sea and the fishing came Támatéa the fair,
Urging his boat to the beach, and the mother awaited him there,
—"Long may you live!" said she.   "Your fishing has sped to a wish.
And now let us choose for the king the fairest of all your fish.

For fear inhabits the palace and grudging grows in
  the land,
Marked is the sluggardly foot and marked the nig-
  gardly hand,
The hours and the miles are counted, the tributes
  numbered and weighed,
And woe to him that comes short, and woe to him
  that delayed!"

So spoke on the beach the mother, and counselled the
  wiser thing.
For Rahéro stirred in the country and secretly mined
  the king.
Nor were the signals wanting of how the leaven
  wrought,
In the cords of obedience loosed and the tributes
  grudgingly brought.
And when last to the temple of Oro the boat with the
  victim sped,
And the priest uncovered the basket and looked on
  the face of the dead,
Trembling fell upon all at sight of an ominous thing,
For there was the aito [1] dead, and he of the house of
  the king.

So spoke on the beach the mother, matter worthy of
  note,
And wattled a basket well, and chose a fish from the
  boat;
And Támatéa the pliable shouldered the basket and
  went,

And travelled, and sang as he travelled, a lad that was
well content.

Still the way of his going was round by the roaring
coast,

Where the ring of the reef is broke and the trades
run riot the most.

On his left, with smoke as of battle, the billows bat-
tered the land;

Unscalable, turreted mountains rose on the inner
hand.

And cape, and village, and river, and vale, and moun-
tain above,

Each had a name in the land for men to remember
and love;

And never the name of a place, but lo! a song in its
praise:

Ancient and unforgotten, songs of the earlier days,

That the elders taught to the young, and at night, in
the full of the moon,

Garlanded boys and maidens sang together in tune.

Támatéa the placable went with a lingering foot;

He sang as loud as a bird, he whistled hoarse as a
flute;

He broiled in the sun, he breathed in the grateful
shadow of trees,

In the icy stream of the rivers he waded over the
knees;

And still in his empty mind crowded, a thousand-fold,

The deeds of the strong and the songs of the cunning
heroes of old.

And now was he come to a place Taiárapu honoured the most,

Where a silent valley of woods debouched on the noisy coast,

Spewing a level river. There was a haunt of Pai.[2]

There, in his potent youth, when his parents drove him to die,

Honoura lived like a beast, lacking the lamp and the fire,

Washed by the rains of the trade and clotting his hair in the mire;

And there, so mighty his hands, he bent the tree to his foot—

So keen the spur of his hunger, he plucked it naked of fruit.

There, as she pondered the clouds for the shadow of coming ills,

Ahupu, the woman of song, walked on high on the hills.

Of these was Rahéro sprung, a man of a godly race;

And inherited cunning of spirit and beauty of body and face.

Of yore in his youth, as an aito, Rahéro wandered the land,

Delighting maids with his tongue, smiting men with his hand.

Famous he was in his youth; but before the midst of his life

Paused, and fashioned a song of farewell to glory and strife.

House of mine (it went), house upon the sea
Belov'd of all my fathers, more belov'd by me!
Vale of the strong Honoura, deep ravine of Pai,
Again in your woody summits I hear the trade-
    wind cry.

House of mine, in your walls, strong sounds the
    sea,
Of all sounds on earth, dearest sound to me.
I have heard the applause of men, I have heard it
    arise and die:
Sweeter now in my house I hear the trade-wind
    cry.

These were the words of his singing, other the
    thought of his heart;
For secret desire of glory vexed him, dwelling apart.
Lazy and crafty he was, and loved to lie in the sun,
And loved the cackle of talk and the true word uttered
    in fun;
Lazy, he was, his roof was ragged, his table was lean,
And the fish swam safe in his sea, and he gathered
    the near and the green.
He sat in his house and laughed, but he loathed the
    king of the land,
And he uttered the grudging word under the cover-
    ing hand.
Treason spread from his door; and he looked for a
    day to come,
A day of the crowding people, a day of the summon-
    ing drum,

When the vote should be taken, the king be driven
    forth in disgrace,
And Rahéro, the laughing and lazy, sit and rule in his
    place.
Here Támatéa came, and beheld the house on the
    brook;
And Rahéro was there by the way and covered an
    oven to cook.[3]
Naked he was to the loins, but the tattoo covered the
    lack,
And the sun and the shadow of palms dappled his
    muscular back.
Swiftly he lifted his head at the fall of the coming feet,
And the water sprang in his mouth with a sudden de-
    sire of meat;
For he marked the basket carried, covered from flies
    and the sun;[4]
And Rahéro buried his fire, but the meat in his house
    was done.

Forth he stepped; and took, and delayed the boy, by
    the hand;
And vaunted the joys of meat and the ancient ways of
    the land:
—"Our sires of old in Taiárapu, they that created the
    race,
Ate ever with eager hand, nor regarded season or
    place,
Ate in the boat at the oar, on the way afoot; and at
    night
Arose in the midst of dreams to rummage the house
    for a bite.

It is good for the youth in his turn to follow the way
    of the sire;

And behold how fitting the time! for here do I cover
    my fire."

—"I see the fire for the cooking but never the meat to
    cook,"

Said Támatéa.—"Tut!" said Rahéro. "Here in the
    brook

And there in the tumbling sea, the fishes are thick as
    flies,

Hungry like healthy men, and like pigs for savour and
    size:

Crayfish crowding the river, sea-fish thronging the
    sea."

—"Well it may be," says the other, "and yet be noth-
    ing to me.

Fain would I eat, but alas! I have needful matter in
    hand,

Since I carry my tribute of fish to the jealous king of
    the land."

Now at the word a light sprang into Rahéro's eyes.

"I will gain me a dinner," thought he, "and lend the
    king a surprise."

And he took the lad by the arm, as they stood by the
    side of the track,

And smiled, and rallied, and flattered, and pushed him
    forward and back.

It was "You that sing like a bird, I never have heard
    you sing,"

And "The lands when I was a lad were none so feared
    of a king.

And of what account is an hour, when the heart is empty of guile?
But come, and sit in the house and laugh with the women awhile;
And I will but drop my hook, and behold! the dinner made."

So Támatéa the pliable hung up his fish in the shade
On a tree by the side of the way; and Rahéro carried him in,
Smiling as smiles the fowler when flutters the bird to the gin,
And chose him a shining hook,[5] and viewed it with sedulous eye,
And breathed and burnished it well on the brawn of his naked thigh,
And set a mat for the gull, and made him be merry and bide,
Like a man concerned for his guest, and the fishing, and nothing beside.
Now when Rahéro was forth, he paused and hearkened, and heard
The gull jest in the house and the women laugh at his word;
And stealthily crossed to the side of the way, to the shady place
Where the basket hung on a mango; and craft transfigured his face.
Deftly he opened the basket, and took of the fat of the fish,
The cut of kings and chieftains, enough for a goodly dish.

This he wrapped in a leaf, set on the fire to cook

And buried; and next the marred remains of the tribute he took,

And doubled and packed them well, and covered the basket close

—"There is a buffet, my king," quoth he, "and a nauseous dose!"—

And hung the basket again in the shade, in a cloud of flies,

—"And there is a sauce to your dinner, king of the crafty eyes!"

Soon as the oven was open, the fish smelt excellent good.

In the shade, by the house of Rahéro, down they sat to their food,

And cleared the leaves [6] in silence, or uttered a jest and laughed,

And raising the cocoanut bowls, buried their faces and quaffed.

But chiefly in silence they ate; and soon as the meal was done,

Rahéro feigned to remember and measured the hour by the sun,

And "Támatéa," quoth he, "it is time to be jogging, my lad."

So Támatéa arose, doing ever the thing he was bade,

And carelessly shouldered the basket, and kindly saluted his host;

And again the way of his going was round by the roaring coast.

Long he went; and at length was aware of a pleasant green,

And the stems and shadows of palms, and roofs of lodges between

There sate, in the door of his palace, the king on a kingly seat.

And aitos stood armed around, and the yottowas [7] sat at his feet.

But fear was a worm in his heart: fear darted his eyes;

And he probed men's faces for treasons and pondered their speech for lies.

To him came Támatéa, the basket slung in his hand,

And paid him the due obeisance standing as vassals stand.

In silence hearkened the king, and closed the eyes in his face,

Harbouring odious thoughts and the baseless fears of the base;

In silence accepted the gift and sent the giver away.

So Támatéa departed, turning his back on the day.

And lo! as the king sat brooding, a rumour rose in the crowd;

The yottowas nudged and whispered, the commons murmured aloud;

Tittering fell upon all at sight of the impudent thing,

At the sight of a gift unroyal flung in the face of a king.

And the face of the king turned white and red with anger and shame

In their midst; and the heart in his body was water
    and then was flame;
Till of a sudden, turning, he gripped an aito hard,
A youth that stood with his ómare,[8] one of the daily
    guard,
And spat in his ear a command, and pointed and ut-
    tered a name,
And hid in the shade of the house his impotent anger
    and shame.
Now Támatéa the fool was far on the homeward way,
The rising night in his face, behind him the dying day.
Rahéro saw him go by, and the heart of Rahéro was
    glad,
Devising shame to the king and nowise harm to the
    lad;
And all that dwelt by the way saw and saluted him
    well,
For he had the face of a friend and the news of the
    town to tell;
And pleased with the notice of folk, and pleased that
    his journey was done,
Támatéa drew homeward, turning his back to the
    sun.

And now was the hour of the bath in Taiárapu: far
    and near
The lovely laughter of bathers rose and delighted his
    ear.
Night massed in the valleys; the sun on the mountain
    coast

Struck, end-long; and above the clouds embattled their host,

And glowed and gloomed on the heights; and the heads of the palms were gems,

And far to the rising eve extended the shade of their stems;

And the shadow of Támatéa hovered already at home.

And sudden the sound of one coming and running light as the foam

Struck on his ear; and he turned, and lo! a man on his track,

Girded and armed with an ómare, following hard at his back.

At a bound the man was upon him;—and, or ever a word was said,

The loaded end of the ómare fell and laid him dead.

II. THE VENGING OF TÁMATÉA

THUS was Rahéro's treason; thus and no further it
   sped;
The king sat safe in his palace and a kindly fool was
   dead.

But the mother of Támatéa arose with death in her
   eyes.
All night long, and the next, Taiárapu rang with her
   cries.
As when a babe in the wood turns with a chill of
   doubt
And perceives nor home, nor friends, for the trees
   have closed her about,
The mountain rings and her breast is torn with the
   voice of despair:
So the lion-like woman idly wearied the air
For awhile, and pierced men's hearing in vain, and
   wounded their hearts.
But as when the weather changes at sea, in danger-
   ous parts,
And sudden the hurricane wrack unrolls up the front
   of the sky,
At once the ship lies idle, the sails hang silent on high,
The breath of the wind that blew is blown out like
   the flame of a lamp,
And the silent armies of death draw near with in-
   audible tramp:
So sudden, the voice of her weeping ceased; in silence
   she rose

And passed from the house of her sorrow, a woman
  clothed with repose,
Carrying death in her breast and sharpening death
  with her hand.

Hither she went and thither in all the coasts of the
  land.
They tell that she feared not to slumber alone, in the
  dead of night,
In accursed places; beheld, unblenched, the ribbon of
  light [9]
Spin from temple to temple; guided the perilous skiff,
Abhorred not the paths of the mountain and trod the
  verge of the cliff;
From end to end of the island, though not the dis-
  tance long,
But forth from king to king carried the tale of her
  wrong.
To king after king, as they sat in the palace door, she
  came,
Claiming kinship, declaiming verses, naming her
  name
And the names of all of her fathers; and still, with a
  heart on the rack,
Jested to capture a hearing and laughed when they
  jested back:
So would deceive them awhile, and change and return
  in a breath,
And on all the men of Vaiau imprecate instant death;
And tempt her kings—for Vaiau was a rich and pros-
  perous land,

And flatter—for who would attempt it but warriors
mighty of hand?

And change in a breath again and rise in a strain of
song,

Invoking the beaten drums, beholding the fall of the
strong,

Calling the fowls of the air to come and feast on the
dead.

And they held the chin in silence, and heard her, and
shook the head;

For they knew the men of Taiárapu famous in battle
and feast,

Marvellous eaters and smiters: the men of Vaiau not
least.

To the land of the Námunu-úra,[10] to Paea, at length
she came,

To men who were foes to the Tevas and hated their
race and name.

There was she well received, and spoke with Hiopa
the king.[11]

And Hiopa listened, and weighed, and wisely con-
sidered the thing.

"Here in the back of the isle we dwell in a sheltered
place,"

Quoth he to the woman, "in quiet, a weak and peace-
able race.

But far in the teeth of the wind lofty Taiárapu lies;

Strong blows the wind of the trade on its seaward
face, and cries

Aloud in the top of arduous mountains, and utters its
song

In green continuous forests.   Strong is the wind, and strong

And fruitful and hardy the race, famous in battle and feast,

Marvellous eaters and smiters: the men of Vaiau not least.

Now hearken to me, my daughter, and hear a word of the wise:

How a strength goes linked with a weakness, two by two, like the eyes.

They can wield the ómare well and cast the javelin far;

Yet are they greedy and weak as the swine and the children are.

Plant we, then, here at Paea, a garden of excellent fruits;

Plant we bananas and kava and taro, the king of roots;

Let the pigs in Paea be tapu [12] and no man fish for a year;

And of all the meat in Tahiti gather we threefold here.

So shall the fame of our plenty fill the island, and so,

At last, on the tongue of rumour, go where we wish it to go.

Then shall the pigs of Taiárapu raise their snouts in the air;

But we sit quiet and wait, as the fowler sits by the snare,

And tranquilly fold our hands, till the pigs come nosing the food:

But meanwhile build us a house of Trotéa, the stub-
    born wood,

Bind it with incombustible thongs, set a roof to the
    room,

Too strong for the hands of a man to dissever or fire
    to consume;

And there, when the pigs come trotting, there shall
    the feast be spread,

There shall the eye of the morn enlighten the feasters
    dead.

So be it done; for I have a heart that pities your state,

And Nateva and Námunu-úra are fire and water for
    hate."

All was done as he said, and the gardens prospered;
    and now

The fame of their plenty went out, and word of it
    came to Vaiau.

For the men of Námunu-úra sailed, to the windward
    far,

Lay in the offing by south where the towns of the
    Tevas are,

And cast overboard of their plenty; and lo! at the
    Tevas' feet

The surf on all of the beaches tumbled treasures of
    meat.

In the salt of the sea, a harvest tossed with the ref-
    luent foam;

And the children gleaned it in playing, and ate and
    carried it home;

And the elders stared and debated, and wondered and passed the jest,

But whenever a guest came by eagerly questioned the guest;

And little by little, from one to another, the word went round:

"In all the borders of Paea the victual rots on the ground,

And swine are plenty as rats. And now, when they fare to the sea,

The men of the Námunu-úra glean from under the tree

And load the canoe to the gunwale with all that is toothsome to eat;

And all day long on the sea the jaws are crushing the meat,

The steersman eats at the helm, the rowers munch at the oar,

And at length, when their bellies are full, overboard with the store!"

Now was the word made true, and soon as the bait was bare,

All the pigs of Taiárapu raised their snouts in the air.

Songs were recited, and kinship was counted, and tales were told

How war had severed of late but peace had cemented of old

The clans of the island. "To war," said they, "now set we an end,

And hie to the Námunu-úra even as a friend to a friend."

So judged, and a day was named; and soon as the
 morning broke,

Canoes were thrust in the sea and the houses emptied
 of folk.

Strong blew the wind of the south, the wind that
 gathers the clan;

Along all the line of the reef the clamorous surges
 ran;

And the clouds were piled on the top of the island
 mountain-high,

A mountain throned on a mountain. The fleet of
 canoes swept by

In the midst, on the green lagoon, with a crew re-
 leased from care,

Sailing an even water, breathing a summer air,

Cheered by a cloudless sun; and ever to left and right,

Bursting surge on the reef, drenching storms on the
 height.

So the folk of Vaiau sailed and were glad all day,

Coasting the palm-tree cape and crossing the popu-
 lous bay

By all the towns of the Tevas; and still as they bowled
 along,

Boat would answer to boat with jest and laughter and
 song,

And the people of all the towns trooped to the sides
 of the sea

And gazed from under the hand or sprang aloft on
 the tree,

Hailing and cheering. Time failed them for more to
 do;

The holiday village careened to the wind, and was gone from view
Swift as a passing bird; and ever as onward it bore,
Like the cry of the passing bird, bequeathed its song to the shore—
Desirable laughter of maids and the cry of delight of the child.
And the gazer, left behind, stared at the wake and smiled.
By all the towns of the Tevas they went, and Pápara last,
The home of the chief, the place of muster in war; and passed
The march of the lands of the clan, to the lands of an alien folk.
And there, from the dusk of the shoreside palms, a column of smoke
Mounted and wavered and died in the gold of the setting sun,
"Paea!" they cried. "It is Paea." And so was the voyage done.

In the early fall of the night, Hiopa came to the shore,
And beheld and counted the comers, and lo, there were forty score:
The pelting feet of the babes that ran already and played,
The clean-lipped smile of the boy, the slender breasts of the maid,
And the mighty limbs of women, stalwart mothers of men.

The sires stood forth unabashed; but a little back
    from his ken
Clustered the scarcely nubile, the lads and maids, in
    a ring,
Fain of each other, afraid of themselves, aware of the
    king
And aping behaviour, but clinging together with
    hands and eyes,
With looks that were kind like kisses, and laughter
    tender as sighs.
There, too, the grandsire stood, raising his silver
    crest,
And the impotent hands of a suckling groped in his
    barren breast.
The childhood of love, the pair well married, the in-
    nocent brood,
The tale of the generations repeated and ever re-
    newed—
Hiopa beheld them together, all the ages of man,
And a moment shook in his purpose.

                But these were the foes of his clan,
And he trod upon pity, and came, and civilly greeted
    the king,
And gravely entreated Rahéro; and for all that could
    fight or sing,
And claimed a name in the land, had fitting phrases
    of praise;
But with all who were well-descended he spoke of
    the ancient days.
And "'Tis true," said he, "that in Paea the victual
    rots on the ground;

But, friends, your number is many; and pigs must be
  hunted and found,
And the lads troop to the mountains to bring the féis
  down,
And around the bowls of the kava cluster the maids
  of the town.
So, for to-night, sleep here; but king, common, and
  priest
To-morrow, in order due, shall sit with me in the
  feast."
Sleepless the live-long night, Hiopa's followers toiled.
The pigs screamed and were slaughtered; the spars
  of the guest-house oiled,
The leaves spread on the floor. In many a mountain
  glen
The moon drew shadows of trees on the naked bodies
  of men
Plucking and bearing fruits; and in all the bounds of
  the town
Red glowed the cocoanut fires and were buried and
  trodden down.
Thus did seven of the yottowas toil with their tale of
  the clan,
But the eighth wrought with his lads, hid from the
  sight of man.
In the deeps of the woods they laboured, piling the
  fuel high
In fagots, the load of a man, fuel seasoned and dry,
Thirsty to seize upon fire and apt to blurt into flame.

And now was the day of the feast. The forests, as
  morning came,

Tossed in the wind, and the peaks quaked in the blaze
of the day

And the cocoanuts showered on the ground, re-
bounding and rolling away:

A glorious morn for a feast, a famous wind for a fire.

To the hall of feasting Hiopa led them, mother and
sire

And maid and babe in a tale, the whole of the holiday
throng.

Smiling they came, garlanded green, not dreaming of
wrong;

And for every three, a pig tenderly cooked in the
ground,

Waited; and féi, the staff of life, heaped in a mound

For each where he sat;—for each, bananas roasted
and raw

Piled with a bountiful hand, as for horses hay and
straw

Are stacked in a stable; and fish, the food of desire,[18]

And plentiful vessels of sauce, and breadfruit gilt in
the fire;—

And kava was common as water. Feasts have there
been ere now,

And many, but never a feast like that of the folk of
Vaiau.

All day long they ate with the resolute greed of
brutes,

And turned from the pigs to the fish, and again from
the fish to the fruits,

And emptied the vessels of sauce, and drank of the
kava deep;

Till the young lay stupid as stones, and the strongest
    nodded to sleep.

Sleep that was mighty as death and blind as a moon-
    less night

Tethered them hand and foot; and their souls were
    drowned, and the light

Was cloaked from their eyes. Senseless together, the
    old and the young,

The fighter deadly to smite and the prater cunning
    of tongue,

The woman wedded and fruitful, inured to the pangs
    of birth,

And the maid that knew not of kisses, blindly
    sprawled on the earth.

From the hall Hiopa the king and his chiefs came
    stealthily forth.

Already the sun hung low and enlightened the peaks
    of the north;

But the wind was stubborn to die and blew as it blows
    at morn,

Showering the nuts in the dusk, and e'en as a banner
    is torn,

High on the peaks of the island, shattered the moun-
    tain cloud.

And now at once, at a signal, a silent, emulous crowd

Set hands to the work of death, hurrying to and fro,

Like ants, to furnish the fagots, building them broad
    and low,

And piling them high and higher around the walls of
    the hall.

Silence persisted within, for sleep lay heavy on all;

But the mother of Támatéa stood at Hiopa's side,
And shook for terror and joy like a girl that is a bride.
Night fell on the toilers, and first Hiopa the wise
Made the round of the house, visiting all with his
eyes;
And all was piled to the eaves, and fuel blockaded the
door;
And within, in the house beleaguered, slumbered the
forty score.
Then was an aito dispatched and came with fire in
his hand,
And Hiopa took it.—"Within," said he, "is the life of
a land;
And behold! I breathe on the coal, I breathe on the
dales of the east,
And silence falls on forest and shore; the voice of the
feast
Is quenched, and the smoke of cooking; the rooftree
decays and falls
On the empty lodge, and the winds subvert deserted
walls."

Therewithal, to the fuel, he laid the glowing coal;
And the redness ran in the mass and burrowed within
like a mole,
And copious smoke was conceived. But, as when a
dam is to burst,
The water lips it and crosses in silver trickles at first,
And then, of a sudden, whelms and bears it away
forthright:
So now, in a moment, the flames sprang and towered
in the night,

And wrestled and roared in the wind, and high over
  house and tree,
Stood, like a streaming torch, enlightening land and
  sea.

But the mother of Támatéa threw her arms abroad,
"Pyre of my son," she shouted, "debited vengeance
  of God,
Late, late, I behold you, yet I behold you at last,
And glory, beholding! For now are the days of my
  agony past,
The lust that famished my soul now eats and drinks
  its desire,
And they that encompassed my son shrivel alive in
  the fire.
Tenfold precious the vengeance that comes after lin-
  gering years!
Ye quenched the voice of my singer?—hark, in your
  dying ears,
The song of the conflagration! Ye left me a widow
  alone?
—Behold, the whole of your race consumes, sinew
  and bone
And torturing flesh together: man, mother, and maid
Heaped in a common shambles; and already, borne
  by the trade,
The smoke of your dissolution darkens the stars of
  night."

Thus she spoke, and her stature grew in the people's
  sight.

III. RAHÉRO

RAHÉRO was there in the hall asleep: beside him
  his wife,
Comely, a mirthful woman, one that delighted in life;
And a girl that was ripe for marriage, shy and sly as
  a mouse;
And a boy, a climber of trees; all the hopes of his
  house.
Unwary, with open hands, he slept in the midst of his
  folk,
And dreamed that he heard a voice crying without,
  and awoke,
Leaping blindly afoot like one from a dream that he
  fears.
A hellish glow and clouds were about him;—it roared
  in his ears
Like the sound of the cataract fall that plunges sud-
  den and steep;
And Rahéro swayed as he stood, and his reason was
  still asleep.
Now the flame struck hard on the house, wind-
  wielded, a fracturing blow,
And the end of the roof was burst and fell on the
  sleepers below;
And the lofty hall, and the feast, and the prostrate
  bodies of folk,
Shone red in his eyes a moment, and then were swal-
  lowed of smoke.
In the mind of Rahéro clearness came; and he
  opened his throat;

And as when a squall comes sudden, the straining sail
of a boat
Thunders aloud and bursts, so thundered the voice of
the man.
—"The wind and the rain!" he shouted, the muster-
ing word of the clan,[14]
And "up!" and "to arms, men of Vaiau!" But silence
replied,
Or only the voice of the gusts of the fire, and nothing
beside.

Rahéro stooped and groped. He handled his woman-
kind,
But the fumes of the fire and the kava had quenched
the life of their mind,
And they lay like pillars prone; and his hand en-
countered the boy,
And there sprang in the gloom of his soul a sudden
lightning of joy.
"Him can I save!" he thought, "if I were speedy
enough."
And he loosened the cloth from his loins, and swad-
dled the child in the stuff;
And about the strength of his neck he knotted the
burden well.

There where the roof had fallen, it roared like the
mouth of hell.
Thither Rahéro went, stumbling on senseless folk,
And grappled a post of the house, and began to climb
in the smoke:

The last alive of Vaiau; and the son borne by the
    sire.

The post glowed in the grain with ulcers of eating
    fire,

And the fire bit to the blood and mangled his hands
    and thighs;

And the fumes sang in his head like wine and stung
    in his eyes;

And still he climbed, and came to the top, the place
    of proof,

And thrust a hand through the flame, and clambered
    alive on the roof.

But even as he did so, the wind, in a garment of
    flames and pain,

Wrapped him from head to heel; and the waistcloth
    parted in twain;

And the living fruit of his loins dropped in the fire
    below.

About the blazing feast-house clustered the eyes of
    the foe,

Watching, hand upon weapon, lest ever a soul should
    flee,

Shading the brow from the glare, straining the neck
    to see.

Only, to leeward, the flames in the wind swept far and
    wide,

And the forest sputtered on fire; and there might no
    man abide.

Thither Rahéro crept, and dropped from the burning
    eaves,

And crouching low to the ground, in a treble covert
    of leaves
And fire and volleying smoke, ran for the life of his
    soul
Unseen; and behind him under a furnace of ardent
    coal,
Cairned with a wonder of flame, and blotting the
    night with smoke,
Blazed and were smelted together the bones of all his
    folk.

He fled unguided at first; but hearing the breakers
    roar,
Thitherward shaped his way, and came at length to
    the shore.
Sound-limbed he was: dry-eyed; but smarted in every
    part;
And the mighty cage of his ribs heaved on his strain-
    ing heart
With sorrow and rage. And "Fools!" he cried, "fools
    of Vaiau,
Heads of swine—gluttons—Alas! and where are they
    now?
Those that I played with, those that nursed me, those
    that I nursed?
God, and I outliving them! I, the least and the
    worst—
I, that thought myself crafty, snared by this herd of
    swine,
In the tortures of hell and desolate, stripped of all
    that was mine:

All!—my friends and my fathers—the silver heads of
  yore
That trooped to the council, the children that ran to
  the open door
Crying with innocent voices and clasping a father's
  knees!
And mine, my wife—my daughter—my sturdy
  climber of trees,
Ah, never to climb again!"

        Thus in the dusk of the night,
(For clouds rolled in the sky and the moon was
  swallowed from sight,)
Pacing and gnawing his fists, Rahéro raged by the
  shore.
Vengeance: that must be his. But much was to do
  before;
And first a single life to be snatched from a deadly
  place,
A life, the root of revenge, surviving plant of the race:
And next the race to be raised anew, and the lands
  of the clan
Repeopled. So Rahéro designed, a prudent man
Even in wrath, and turned for the means of revenge
  and escape:
A boat to be seized by stealth, a wife to be taken by
  rape.

Still was the dark lagoon; beyond on the coral wall,
He saw the breakers shine, he heard them bellow and
  fall.

Alone, on the top of the reef, a man with a flaming brand

Walked, gazing and pausing, a fish-spear poised in his hand.

The foam boiled to his calf when the mightier breakers came,

And the torch shed in the wind scattering tufts of flame.

Afar on the dark lagoon a canoe lay idly at wait:

A figure dimly guiding it: surely the fisherman's mate.

Rahéro saw and smiled. He straightened his mighty thews:

Naked, with never a weapon, and covered with scorch and bruise,

He straightened his arms, he filled the void of his body with breath,

And, strong as the wind in his manhood, doomed the fisher to death.

Silent he entered the water, and silently swam, and came

There where the fisher walked, holding on high the flame.

Loud on the pier of the reef volleyed the breach of the sea;

And hard at the back of the man, Rahéro crept to his knee

On the coral, and suddenly sprang and seized him, the elder hand

Clutching the joint of his throat, the other snatching the brand

Ere it had time to fall, and holding it steady and high.
Strong was the fisher, brave and swift of mind and of
  eye—
Strongly he threw in the clutch; but Rahéro resisted
  the strain,
And jerked, and the spine of life snapped with a crack
  in twain,
And the man came slack in his hands and tumbled a
  lump at his feet.

One moment: and there, on the reef, where the break-
  ers whitened and beat,
Rahéro was standing alone, glowing and scorched
  and bare,
A victor unknown of any, raising the torch in the air.
But once he drank of his breath, and instantly set him
  to fish
Like a man intent upon supper at home and a savoury
  dish.
For what should the woman have seen?   A man with
  a torch—and then
A moment's blur of the eyes—and a man with a torch
  again.
And the torch had scarcely been shaken.   "Ah,
  surely," Rahéro said,
"She will deem it a trick of the eyes, a fancy born in
  the head;
But time must be given the fool to nourish a fool's
  belief."
So for a while, a sedulous fisher, he walked the reef,
Pausing at times and gazing, striking at times with
  the spear:

—Lastly, uttered the call; and even as the boat drew
 near,
Like a man that was done with its use, tossed the
 torch in the sea.

Lightly he leaped on the boat beside the woman; and
 she
Lightly addressed him, and yielded the paddle and
 place to sit;
For now the torch was extinguished the night was
 black as the pit.
Rahéro set him to row, never a word he spoke,
And the boat sang in the water urged by his vigorous
 stroke.
—"What ails you?" the woman asked, "and why did
 you drop the brand?
We have only to kindle another as soon as we come
 to land."
Never a word Rahéro replied, but urged the canoe.
And a chill fell on the woman.—"Atta! speak! is it
 you?
Speak! Why are you silent? Why do you bend
 aside?
Wherefore steer to the seaward?" thus she panted
 and cried.
Never a word from the oarsman, toiling there in the
 dark;
But right for a gate of the reef he silently headed the
 bark,
And wielding the single paddle with passionate sweep
 on sweep,

Drove her, the little fitted, forth on the open deep.

And fear, there where she sat, froze the woman to stone:

Not fear of the crazy boat and the weltering deep alone;

But a keener fear of the night, the dark, and the ghostly hour,

And the thing that drove the canoe with more than a mortal's power

And more than a mortal's boldness. For much she knew of the dead

That haunt and fish upon reefs, toiling, like men, for bread,

And traffic with human fishers, or slay them and take their ware,

Till the hour when the star of the dead [15] grows down, and the morning air

Blows, and the cocks are singing on shore. And surely she knew.

The speechless thing at her side belonged to the grave. [16]

                                        It blew

All night from the south; all night, Rahéro contended and kept

The prow to the cresting sea; and, silent, as though she slept,

The woman huddled and quaked. And now was the peek of day.

High and long on their left the mountainous island lay;

And over the peaks of Taiárapu arrows of sunlight
struck.

On shore the birds were beginning to sing: the
ghostly ruck

Of the buried had long ago returned to the covered
grave;

And here on the sea, the woman, waxing suddenly
brave,

Turned her swiftly about and looked in the face of
the man.

And sure he was none that she knew, none of her
country or clan:

A stranger, mother-naked, and marred with the
marks of fire,

But comely and great of stature, a man to obey and
admire.

And Rahéro regarded her also, fixed, with a frowning
face,

Judging the woman's fitness to mother a warlike race.

Broad of shoulder, ample of girdle, long in the thigh,

Deep of bosom she was, and bravely supported his
eye.

"Woman," said he, "last night the men of your folk—

Man, woman, and maid, smothered my race in smoke.

It was done like cowards: and I, a mighty man of my
hands,

Escaped, a single life; and now to the empty lands

And smokeless hearths of my people, sail, with your-
self, alone.

Before your mother was born, the die of to-day was
  thrown
And you selected:—your husband, vainly striving, to
  fall
Broken between these hands:—yourself to be severed
  from all,
The places, the people, you love—home, kindred, and
  clan—
And to dwell in a desert and bear the babes of a kin-
  less man."

THE FEAST OF FAMINE

I. THE PRIEST'S VIGIL

IN all the land of the tribe was neither fish nor fruit,
And the deepest pit of popoi stood empty to the foot.[1]
The clans upon the left and the clans upon the right
Now oiled their carven maces and scoured their daggers bright;
They gat them to the thicket, to the deepest of the shade,
And lay with sleepless eyes in the deadly ambuscade.
And oft in the starry even the song of morning rose,
What time the oven smoked in the country of their foes;
For oft to loving hearts, and waiting ears and sight,
The lads that went to forage returned not with the night.
Now first the children sickened, and then the women paled,
And the great arms of the warrior no more for war availed.
Hushed was the deep drum, discarded was the dance;
And those that met the priest now glanced at him askance.
The priest was a man of years, his eyes were ruby-red,[2]
He neither feared the dark nor the terrors of the dead,

He knew the songs of races, the names of ancient
    date;

And the beard upon his bosom would have bought
    the chief's estate.

He dwelt in a high-built lodge, hard by the roaring
    shore,

Raised on a noble terrace and with tikis[3] at the door.

Within it was full of riches, for he served his nation
    well,

And full of the sound of breakers, like the hollow of
    a shell.

For weeks he let them perish, gave never a helping
    sign,

But sat on his oiled platform to commune with the
    divine,

But sat on his high terrace, with the tikis by his side,

And stared on the blue ocean, like a parrot, ruby-
    eyed.

Dawn as yellow as sulphur leaped on the mountain
    height;

Out on the round of the sea the gems of the morning
    light,

Up from the round of the sea the streamers of the
    sun;—

But down in the depths of the valley the day was not
    begun.

In the blue of the woody twilight burned red the
    cocoahusk,

And the women and men of the clan went forth to
    bathe in the dusk,

A word that began to go round, a word, a whisper, a
    start:
Hope that leaped in the bosom, fear that knocked on
    the heart:
"See, the priest is not risen—look, for his door is fast!
He is going to name the victims; he is going to help
    us at last."

Thrice rose the sun to noon; and ever, like one of the
    dead,
The priest lay still in his house with the roar of the
    sea in his head;
There was never a foot on the floor, there was never
    a whisper of speech;
Only the leering tikis stared on the blinding beach.
Again were the mountains fired, again the morning
    broke;
And all the houses lay still, but the house of the priest
    awoke.
Close in their covering roofs lay and trembled the
    clan,
But the agèd, red-eyed priest ran forth like a lunatic
    man;
And the village panted to see him in the jewels of
    death again,
In the silver beards of the old and the hair of women
    slain.
Frenzy shook in his limbs, frenzy shone in his eyes,
And still and again as he ran, the valley rang with his
    cries.
All day long in the land, by cliff and thicket and den,

He ran his lunatic rounds, and howled for the flesh of
    men;
All day long he ate not, nor ever drank of the brook;
And all day long in their houses the people listened
    and shook—
All day long in their houses they listened with bated
    breath,
And never a soul went forth, for the sight of the priest
    was death.

Three were the days of his running, as the gods ap-
    pointed of yore,
Two the nights of his sleeping alone in the place of
    gore:
The drunken slumber of frenzy twice he drank to the
    lees,
On the sacred stones of the High-place under the
    sacred trees;
With a lamp at his ashen head he lay in the place of
    the feast,
And the sacred leaves of the banyan rustled around
    the priest.
Last, when the stated even fell upon terrace and tree,
And the shade of the lofty island lay leagues away to
    sea,
And all the valleys of verdure were heavy with manna
    and musk,
The wreck of the red-eyed priest came gasping home
    in the dusk.
He reeled across the village, he staggered along the
    shore,

And between the leering tikis crept groping through
    his door.

There went a stir through the lodges, the voice of
    speech awoke;

Once more from the builded platforms arose the
    evening smoke.

And those who were mighty in war, and those re-
    nowned for an art

Sat in their stated seats and talked of the morrow
    apart.

II. THE LOVERS

HARK! away in the woods—for the ears of love are sharp—
Stealthily, quietly touched, the note of the one-stringed harp.[4]
In the lighted house of her father, why should Taheia start?
Taheia heavy of hair, Taheia tender of heart,
Taheia the well-descended, a bountiful dealer in love,
Nimble of foot like the deer, and kind of eye like the dove?
Sly and shy as a cat, with never a change of face,
Taheia slips to the door, like one that would breathe a space;
Saunters and pauses, and looks at the stars, and lists to the seas;
Then sudden and swift as a cat, she plunges under the trees.
Swift as a cat she runs, with her garment gathered high,
Leaping, nimble of foot, running, certain of eye;
And ever to guide her way over the smooth and the sharp,
Ever nearer and nearer the note of the one-stringed harp;
Till at length, in a glade of the wood, with a naked mountain above,
The sound of the harp thrown down, and she in the arms of her love.

"Rua,"—"Taheia," they cry—"my heart, my soul, and
my eyes,"
And clasp and sunder and kiss, with lovely laughter
and sighs,
"Rua!"—"Taheia, my love,"—"Rua, star of my night,
Clasp me, hold me, and love me, single spring of de-
light."

And Rua folded her close, he folded her near and long,
The living knit to the living, and sang the lover's
song:

> *Night, night it is, night upon the palms.*
> *Night, night it is, the land wind has blown.*
> *Starry, starry night, over deep and height;*
> *Love, love in the valley, love all alone.*

"Taheia, heavy of hair, a foolish thing have we done,
To bind what gods have sundered unkindly into one.
Why should a lowly lover have touched Taheia's
skirt,
Taheia the well-descended, and Rua child of the
dirt?"

"—On high with the haka-ikis my father sits in state,
Ten times fifty kinsmen salute him in the gate;
Round all his martial body, and in bands across his
face,
The marks of the tattooer proclaim his lofty place.
I too, in the hands of the cunning, in the sacred cabin
of palm,[5]

Have shrunk like the mimosa, and bleated like the
    lamb;
Round half my tender body, that none shall clasp but
    you,
For a crest and a fair adornment go dainty lines of
    blue.
Love, love, beloved Rua, love levels all degrees,
And the well-tattooed Taheia clings panting to your
    knees."

"—Taheia, song of the morning, how long is the long-
    est love?
A cry, a clasp of the hands, a star that falls from
    above!
Ever at morn in the blue, and at night when all is
    black,
Ever it skulks and trembles with the hunter, Death,
    on its track.
Hear me, Taheia, death! For to-morrow the priest
    shall awake,
And the names be named of the victims to bleed for
    the nation's sake;
And first of the numbered many that shall be slain
    ere noon,
Rua the child of the dirt, Rua the kinless loon.
For him shall the drum be beat, for him be raised the
    song,
For him to the sacred High-place the chaunting peo-
    ple throng,
For him the oven smoke as for a speechless beast,
And the sire of my Taheia come greedy to the feast."

"Rua, be silent, spare me.   Taheia closes her ears.
Pity my yearning heart, pity my girlish years!
Flee from the cruel hands, flee from the knife and
    coal,
Lie hid in the deeps of the woods, Rua, sire of my
    soul!"

"Whither to flee, Taheia, whither in all of the land?
The fires of the bloody kitchen are kindled on every
    hand;
On every hand in the isle a hungry whetting of teeth,
Eyes in the trees above, arms in the brush beneath.
Patience to lie in wait, cunning to follow the sleuth,
Abroad the foes I have fought, and at home the
    friends of my youth."

"Love, love, beloved Rua, love has a clearer eye,
Hence from the arms of love you go not forth to die.
There, where the broken mountain drops sheer into
    the glen.
There shall you find a hold from the boldest hunter of
    men;
There, in the deep recess, where the sun falls only at
    noon,
And only once in the night enters the light of the
    moon,
Nor ever a sound but of birds, or the rain when it
    falls with a shout;
For death and the fear of death beleaguer the valley
    about.
Tapu it is, but the gods will surely pardon despair;
Tapu, but what of that?   If Rua can only dare.

Tapu and tapu and tapu, I know they are every one
    right;
But the god of every tapu is not always quick to
    smite.
Lie secret there, my Rua, in the arms of awful gods,
Sleep in the shade of the trees on the couch of the
    kindly sods,
Sleep and dream of Taheia, Taheia will wake for you;
And whenever the land wind blows and the woods
    are heavy with dew,
Alone through the horror of night,[6] with food for the
    soul of her love,
Taheia the undissuaded will hurry true as the dove."

"Taheia, the pit of the night crawls with treacherous
    things,
Spirits of ultimate air and the evil souls of things;
The souls of the dead, the stranglers, that perch in
    the trees of the wood,
Waiters for all things human, haters of evil and
    good."
"Rua, behold me, kiss me, look in my eyes and read;
Are these the eyes of a maid that would leave her
    lover in need?
Brave in the eye of the day, my father ruled in the
    fight;
The child of his loins, Taheia, will play the man in the
    night."

So it was spoken, and so agreed, and Taheia arose
And smiled in the stars and was gone, swift as the
    swallow goes;

And Rua stood on the hill, and sighed, and followed
　　her flight,
And there were lodges below, each with its door
　　alight;
From folk that sat on the terrace and drew out the
　　even long
Sudden crowings of laughter, monotonous drone of
　　song;
The quiet passage of souls over his head in the trees;
And from all around the haven the crumbling thunder
　　of seas.
"Farewell, my home," said Rua. "Farewell, O quiet
　　seat!
To-morrow in all your valleys the drum of death shall
　　beat."

III. THE FEAST

DAWN as yellow as sulphur leaped on the naked
  peak,
And all the village was stirring, for now was the
  priest to speak.
Forth on his terrace he came, and sat with the chief
  in talk;
His lips were blackened with fever, his cheeks were
  whiter than chalk;
Fever clutched at his hands, fever nodded his head,
But, quiet and steady and cruel, his eyes shone ruby-
  red.
In the earliest rays of the sun the chief rose up con-
  tent;
Braves were summoned, and drummers; messengers
  came and went;
Braves ran to their lodges, weapons were snatched
  from the wall;
The commons herded together, and fear was over
  them all.
Festival dresses they wore, but the tongue was dry in
  their mouth,
And the blinking eyes in their faces skirted from
  north to south.

Now to the sacred enclosure gathered the greatest
  and least,
And from under the shade of the banyan arose the
  voice of the feast,

The frenzied roll of the drum, and a swift, monoto-
   nous song.
Higher the sun swam up; the trade wind level and
   strong
Awoke in the tops of the palms and rattled the fans
   aloud,
And over the garlanded heads and shining robes of
   the crowd
Tossed the spiders of shadow, scattered the jewels of
   sun.
Forty the tale of the drums, and the forty throbbed
   like one;
A thousand hearts in the crowd, and the even chorus
   of song,
Swift as the feet of a runner, trampled a thousand
   strong.

And the old men leered at the ovens and licked their
   lips for the food;
And the women stared at the lads, and laughed and
   looked to the wood.
As when the sweltering baker, at night, when the
   city is dead,
Alone in the trough of labour treads and fashions the
   bread;
So in the heat, and the reek, and the touch of woman
   and man,
The naked spirit of evil kneaded the hearts of the
   clan.

Now cold was at many a heart, and shaking in many
   a seat;

For there were the empty baskets, but who was to
    furnish the meat?

For here was the nation assembled, and there were
    the ovens anigh,

And out of a thousand singers nine were numbered to
    die.

Till, of a sudden, a shock, a mace in the air, a yell,

And, struck in the edge of the crowd, the first of the
    victims fell.[8]

Terror and horrible glee divided the shrinking clan,

Terror of what was to follow, glee for a diet of man.

Frenzy hurried the chaunt, frenzy rattled the drums;

The nobles, high on the terrace, greedily mouthed
    their thumbs;

And once and again and again, in the ignorant crowd
    below,

Once and again and again descended the murderous
    blow.

Now smoked the oven, and now, with the cutting lip
    of a shell,

A butcher of ninety winters jointed the bodies well.

Unto the carven lodge, silent, in order due,

The grandees of the nation one after one withdrew;

And a line of laden bearers brought to the terrace
    foot,

On poles across their shoulders, the last reserve of
    fruit.

The victims bled for the nobles in the old appointed
    way;

The fruit was spread for the commons, for all should
    eat to-day.

And now was the kava brewed, and now the cocoa
   ran,
Now was the hour of the dance for child and woman
   and man;
And mirth was in every heart, and a garland on every
   head,
And all was well with the living and well with the
   eight who were dead.
Only the chiefs and the priest talked and consulted
   awhile:
"To-morrow," they said, and "To-morrow," and
   nodded and seemed to smile:
"Rua the child of dirt, the creature of common clay,
Rua must die to-morrow, since Rua is gone to-day."

Out of the groves of the valley, where clear the black-
   birds sang,
Sheer from the trees of the valley the face of the
   mountain sprang;
Sheer and bare it rose, unscalable barricade,
Beaten and blown against by the generous draught of
   the trade.
Dawn on its fluted brow painted rainbow light,
Close on its pinnacled crown trembled the stars at
   night.
Here and there in a cleft clustered contorted trees,
Or the silver beard of a stream hung and swung in
   the breeze.
High overhead, with a cry, the torrents leaped for
   the main,
And silently sprinkled below in thin perennial rain.

Dark in the staring noon, dark was Rua's ravine,
Damp and cold was the air, and the face of the cliffs
was green.
Here, in the rocky pit, accursed already of old,
On a stone in the midst of a river, Rua sat and was
cold.

"Valley of mid-day shadows, valley of silent falls,"
Rua sang, and his voice went hollow about the walls,
"Valley of shadow and rock, a doleful prison to me.
What is the life you can give to a child of the sun and
the sea?"
And Rua arose and came to the open mouth of the
glen,
Whence he beheld the woods, and the sea, and the
houses of men.
Wide blew the riotous trade, and smelt in his nostrils
good;
It bowed the boats on the bay, and tore and divided
the wood;
It smote and sundered the groves as Moses smote
with the rod;
And the streamers of all the trees blew like banners
abroad;
And ever and on, in a lull, the trade wind brought him
along
A far-off patter of drums and a far-off whisper of
song.

Swift as the swallow's wings, the diligent hands on
the drum

Fluttered and hurried and throbbed. "Ah, woe that I
    hear you come,"
Rua cried in his grief, "a sorrowful sound to me,
Mounting far and faint from the resonant shore of
    the sea!
Woe in the song! for the grave breathes in the
    singers' breath,
And I hear in the tramp of the drums the beat of the
    heart of death.
Home of my youth! no more, through all the length
    of the years,
No more to the place of the echoes of early laughter
    and tears,
No more shall Rua return; no more as the evening
    ends,
To crowded eyes of welcome, to the reaching hands
    of friends."

All day long from the High-place the drums and the
    singing came,
And the even fell, and the sun went down, a wheel of
    flame;
And night came gleaning the shadows and hushing
    the sounds of the wood;
And silence slept on all, where Rua sorrowed and
    stood.
But still from the shore of the bay the sound of the
    festival rang,
And still the crowd in the High-place danced and
    shouted and sang.

Now over all the isle terror was breathed abroad

Of shadowy hands from the trees and shadowy snares
in the sod;

And before the nostrils of night, the shuddering
hunter of men

Hurried, with beard on shoulder, back to his lighted
den.

"Taheia, here to my side!"—"Rua, my Rua, you!"

And cold from the clutch of terror, cold with the
damp of the dew,

Taheia, heavy of hair, leaped through the dark to his
arms;

Taheia leaped to his clasp, and was folded in from
alarms.

"Rua, beloved, here, see what your love has brought;

Coming—alas! returning—swift as the shuttle of
thought;

Returning, alas! for to-night, with the beaten drum
and the voice,

In the shine of many torches must the sleepless clan
rejoice;

And Taheia the well-descended, the daughter of chief
and priest,

Taheia must sit in her place in the crowded bench of
the feast."

So it was spoken; and she, girding her garment
high,

Fled and was swallowed of woods, swift as the sight
of an eye.

Night over isle and sea rolled her curtain of stars,

Then a trouble awoke in the air, the east was banded with bars;

Dawn as yellow as sulphur leaped on the mountain height;

Dawn, in the deepest glen, fell a wonder of light;

High and clear stood the palms in the eye of the brightening east,

And lo! from the sides of the sea the broken sound of the feast!

As, when in days of summer, through open windows, the fly

Swift as a breeze and loud as a trump goes by,

But when frosts in the field have pinched the wintering mouse,

Blindly noses and buzzes and hums in the firelit house:

So the sound of the feast gallantly trampled at night,

So it staggered and drooped, and droned in the morning light.

IV. THE RAID

IT chanced that as Rua sat in the valley of silent falls,
He heard a calling of doves from high on the cliffy
walls.
Fire had fashioned of yore, and time had broken, the
rocks;
There were rooting crannies for trees and nesting-
places for flocks;
And he saw on the top of the cliffs, looking up from
the pit of the shade,
A flicker of wings and sunshine, and trees that swung
in the trade.
"The trees swing in the trade," quoth Rua, doubtful
of words,
"And the sun stares from the sky, but what should
trouble the birds?"
Up from the shade he gazed, where high the parapet
shone,
And he was aware of a ledge and of things that
moved thereon.
"What manner of things are these? Are they spirits
abroad by day?
Or the foes of my clan that are come, bringing death
by a perilous way?"

The valley was gouged like a vessel, and round like
the vessel's lip,
With a cape of the side of the hill thrust forth like
the bows of a ship.

On the top of the face of the cape a volley of sun
    struck fair,
And the cape overhung like a chin a gulph of sunless
    air.
"Silence, heart! What is that?—that, that flickered
    and shone,
Into the sun for an instant, and in an instant gone?
Was it a warrior's plume, a warrior's girdle of hair?
Swung in the loop of a rope, is he making a bridge of
    the air?"

Once and again Rua saw, in the trenchant edge of the
    sky,
The giddy conjuring done. And then, in the blink of
    an eye,
A scream caught in with the breath, a whirling packet
    of limbs,
A lump that dived in the gulph, more swift than a
    dolphin swims;
And there was the lump at his feet, and eyes were
    alive in the lump.
Sick was the soul of Rua, ambushed close in a clump;
Sick of soul he drew near, making his courage stout;
And he looked in the face of the thing, and the life of
    the thing went out.
And he gazed on the tattooed limbs, and, behold, he
    knew the man:
Hoka, a chief of the Vais, the truculent foe of his
    clan:
Hoka a moment since that stepped in the loop of the
    rope,

Filled with the lust of war, and alive with courage and
    hope.

Again to the giddy cornice Rua lifted his eyes
And again beheld men passing in the armpit of the
    skies.
"Foes of my race!" cried Rua, "the mouth of Rua is
    true:
Never a shark in the deep is nobler of soul than you.
There was never a nobler foray, never a bolder plan;
Never a dizzier path was trod by the children of man;
And Rua, your evil-dealer through all the days of his
    years,
"Counts it honour to hate you, honour to fall by your
    spears."

And Rua straightened his back. "O Vais, a scheme
    for a scheme!"
Cried Rua and turned and descended the turbulent
    stair of the stream,
Leaping from rock to rock as the water-wagtail at
    home
Flits through resonant valleys and skims by boulder
    and foam.
And Rua burst from the glen and leaped on the shore
    of the brook,
And straight for the roofs of the clan his vigorous
    way he took.
Swift were the heels of his flight, and loud behind as
    he went
Rattled the leaping stones on the line of his long
    descent.

And ever he thought as he ran, and caught at his gasping breath,
"O the fool of a Rua, Rua that runs to his death!
But the right is the right," thought Rua, and ran like the wind on the foam,
"The right is the right for ever, and home for ever home.
For what though the oven smoke? And what though I die ere morn?
There was I nourished and tended, and there was Taheia born."
Noon was high on the High-place, the second noon of the feast;
And heat and shameful slumber weighed on people and priest;
And the heart drudged slow in bodies heavy with monstrous meals;
And the senseless limbs were scattered abroad like spokes of wheels;
And crapulous women sat and stared at the stones anigh
With a bestial droop of the lip and a swinish rheum in the eye.
As about the dome of the bees in the time for the drones to fall,
The dead and the maimed are scattered, and lie, and stagger, and crawl;
So on the grades of the terrace, in the ardent eye of the day,
The half-awake and the sleepers clustered and crawled and lay;

And loud as the dome of the bees, in the time of a swarming horde,
A horror of many insects hung in the air and roared.
Rua looked and wondered; he said to himself in his heart:
"Poor are the pleasures of life, and death is the better part."
But lo! on the higher benches a cluster of tranquil folk
Sat by themselves, nor raised their serious eyes, nor spoke:
Women with robes unruffled and garlands duly arranged,
Gazing far from the feast with faces of people estranged;
And quiet amongst the quiet, and fairer than all the fair,
Taheia, the well-descended, Taheia, heavy of hair.
And the soul of Rua awoke, courage enlightened his eyes,
And he uttered a summoning shout and called on the clan to rise.
Over against him at once, in the spotted shade of the trees,
Owlish and blinking creatures scrambled to hands and knees;
On the grades of the sacred terrace, the driveller woke to fear,
And the hand of the ham-drooped warrior brandished a wavering spear.
And Rua folded his arms, and scorn discovered his teeth;

Above the war-crowd gibbered, and Rua stood smil-
     ing beneath.
Thick, like leaves in the autumn, faint, like April
     sleet,
Missiles from tremulous hands quivered around his
     feet;
And Taheia leaped from her place; and the priest,
     the ruby-eyed,
Ran to the front of the terrace, and brandished his
     arms, and cried:
"Hold, O fools, he brings tidings!" and "Hold, 'tis the
     love of my heart!"
Till lo! in front of the terrace, Rua pierced with a
     dart.

Taheia cherished his head, and the aged priest stood
     by,
And gazed with eyes of ruby at Rua's darkening
     eye.
"Taheia, here is the end, I die a death for a man.
I have given the life of my soul to save an unsavable
     clan.
See them, the drooping of hams; behold me the blink-
     ing crew:
Fifty spears they cast, and one of fifty true!
And you, O priest, the foreteller, foretell for yourself
     if you can,
Foretell the hour of the day when the Vais shall burst
     on your clan!
By the head of the tapu cleft, with death and fire in
     their hand,

Thick and silent like ants, the warriors swarm in the
land."
And they tell that when next the sun had climbed to
the noonday skies,
It shone on the smoke of feasting in the country of
the Vais.

TICONDEROGA

A LEGEND OF THE WEST HIGHLANDS

THIS is the tale of the man
   Who heard a word in the night
In the land of the heatherly hills,
   In the days of the feud and the fight.
By the sides of the rainy sea,
   Where never a stranger came,
On the awful lips of the dead,
   He heard the outlandish name.
It sang in his sleeping ears,
   It hummed in his waking head:
The name—Ticonderoga,
   The utterance of the dead.

I. THE SAYING OF THE NAME

ON the loch-sides of Appin,
   When the mist blew from the sea,
A Stewart stood with a Cameron:
   An angry man was he.
The blood beat in his ears,
   The blood ran hot to his head,
The mist blew from the sea,
   And there was the Cameron dead.
"O, what have I done to my friend,
   O, what have I done to mysel',
That he should be cold and dead,
   And I in the danger of all?

Nothing but danger about me,
　　Danger behind and before,
Death at wait in the heather
　　In Appin and Mamore,
Hate at all of the ferries
　　And death at each of the fords,
Camerons priming gunlocks
　　And Camerons sharpening swords."

But this was a man of counsel,
　　This was a man of a score,
There dwelt no pawkier Stewart
　　In Appin or Mamore.
He looked on the blowing mist,
　　He looked on the awful dead,
And there came a smile on his face
　　And there slipped a thought in his head.

Out over cairn and moss,
　　Out over scrog and scaur,
He ran as runs the clansman
　　That bears the cross of war.
His heart beat in his body,
　　His hair clove to his face,
When he came at last in the gloaming
　　To the dead man's brother's place.
The east was white with the moon,
　　The west with the sun was red,
And there, in the house-doorway,
　　Stood the brother of the dead.

"I have slain a man to my danger,
   I have slain a man to my death.
I put my soul in your hands,"
   The panting Stewart saith.
"I lay it bare in your hands,
   For I know your hands are leal;
And be you my targe and bulwark
   From the bullet and the steel."

Then up and spoke the Cameron,
   And gave him his hand again:
"There shall never a man in Scotland
   Set faith in me in vain;
And whatever man you have slaughtered,
   Of whatever name or line,
By my sword and yonder mountain,
   I make your quarrel mine.[1]
I bid you in to my fireside,
   I share with you house and hall;
It stands upon my honour
   To see you safe from all."

It fell in the time of midnight,
   When the fox barked in the den
And the plaids were over the faces
   In all the houses of men,
That as the living Cameron
   Lay sleepless on his bed,
Out of the night and the other world,
   Came in to him the dead.

"My blood is on the heather,
　　My bones are on the hill;
There is joy in the home of ravens
　　That the young shall eat their fill.
My blood is poured in the dust,
　　My soul is spilled in the air;
And the man that has undone me
　　Sleeps in my brother's care."

"I'm wae for your death, my brother,
　　But if all of my house were dead,
I couldnae withdraw the plighted hand,
　　Nor break the word once said."

"O, what shall I say to our father,
　　In the place to which I fare?
O, what shall I say to our mother,
　　Who greets to see me there?
And to all the kindly Camerons
　　That have lived and died long-syne—
Is this the word you send them,
　　Fause-hearted brother mine?"

"It's neither fear nor duty,
　　It's neither quick nor dead
Shall gar me withdraw the plighted hand,
　　Or break the word once said."

Thrice in the time of midnight,
　　When the fox barked in the den,
And the plaids were over the faces
　　In all the houses of men,

Thrice as the living Cameron
  Lay sleepless on his bed,
Out of the night and the other world
  Came in to him the dead,
And cried to him for vengeance
  On the man that laid him low;
And thrice the living Cameron
  Told the dead Gameron, no.

"Thrice have you seen me, brother,
  But now shall see me no more,
Till you meet your angry fathers
  Upon the farther shore.
Thrice have I spoken, and now,
  Before the cock be heard,
I take my leave for ever
  With the naming of a word.
It shall sing in your sleeping ears,
  It shall hum in your waking head,
The name—Ticonderoga,
  And the warning of the dead."

Now when the night was over
  And the time of people's fears,
The Cameron walked abroad,
  And the word was in his ears.
"Many a name I know,
  But never a name like this;
O, where shall I find a skilly man
  Shall tell me what it is?"
With many a man he counselled
  Of high and low degree,

With the herdsmen on the mountains
　　And the fishers of the sea.
And he came and went unweary,
　　And read the books of yore,
And the runes that were written of old
　　On the stones upon the moor.
And many a name he was told,
　　But never the name of his fears—
Never, in east or west,
　　The name that rang in his ears:
Names of men and of clans;
　　Names for the grass and the tree,
For the smallest tarn in the mountains,
　　The smallest reef in the sea:
Names for the high and low,
　　The names of the craig and the flat;
But in all the land of Scotland,
　　Never a name like that.

II. THE SEEKING OF THE NAME

AND now there was speech in the south,
  And a man of the south that was wise,
A periwig'd lord of London,[2]
  Called on the clans to rise.
And the riders rode, and the summons
  Came to the western shore,
To the land of the sea and the heather,
  To Appin and Mamore.
It called on all to gather
  From every scrog and scaur,
That loved their fathers' tartan
  And the ancient game of war.
And down the watery valley
  And up the windy hill,
Once more, as in the olden,
  The pipes were sounding shrill;
Again in highland sunshine
  The naked steel was bright;
And the lads, once more in tartan,
  Went forth again to fight.

"O, why should I dwell here
  With a weird upon my life,
When the clansmen shout for battle
  And the war-swords clash in strife?
I cannae joy at feast,
  I cannae sleep in bed,
For the wonder of the word
  And the warning of the dead.
It sings in my sleeping ears
  It hums in my waking head,

The name—Ticonderoga,
  The utterance of the dead.
Then up, and with the fighting men
  To march away from here,
Till the cry of the great war-pipe
  Shall drown it in my ear!"

Where flew King George's ensign
  The plaided soldiers went:
They drew the sword in Germany,
  In Flanders pitched the tent.
The bells of foreign cities
  Rang far across the plain:
They passed the happy Rhine,
  They drank the rapid Main.
Through Asiatic jungles
  The Tartans filed their way,
And the neighing of the warpipes
  Struck terror in Cathay.[3]
"Many a name have I heard," he thought,
  "In all the tongues of men,
Full many a name both here and there,
  Full many both now and then.
When I was at home in my father's house
  In the land of the naked knee,
Between the eagles that fly in the lift
  And the herrings that swim in the sea,
And now that I am a captain-man
  With a braw cockade in my hat—
Many a name have I heard," he thought,
  "But never a name like that."

III. THE PLACE OF THE NAME

THERE fell a war in a woody place,
  Lay far across the sea,
A war of the march in the mirk midnight
  And the shot from behind the tree,
The shaven head and the painted face,
  The silent foot in the wood,
In a land of a strange, outlandish tongue
  That was hard to be understood.

It fell about the gloaming
  The general stood with his staff,
He stood and he looked east and west
  With little mind to laugh.
"Far have I been and much have I seen,
  And kent both gain and loss,
But here we have woods on every hand
  And a kittle water to cross.
Far have I been and much have I seen,
  But never the beat of this;
And there's one must go down to that waterside
  To see how deep it is."

It fell in the dusk of the night
  When unco things betide,
The skilly captain, the Cameron,
  Went down to that waterside.
Canny and soft the captain went;
  And a man of the woody land,
With the shaven head and the painted face,
  Went down at his right hand.

It fell in the quiet night,
   There was never a sound to ken;
But all of the woods to the right and left
   Lay filled with the painted men.

"Far have I been and much have I seen,
   Both as a man and boy,
But never have I set forth a foot
   On so perilous an employ."
It fell in the dusk of the night
   When unco things betide,
That he was aware of a captain-man
   Drew near to the waterside.
He was aware of his coming
   Down in the gloaming alone;
And he looked in the face of the man
   And lo! the face was his own.
"This is my weird," he said,
   "And now I ken the worst;
For many shall fall the morn,
   But I shall fall with the first.
O, you of the outland tongue,
   You of the painted face,
This is the place of my death;
   Can you tell me the name of the place?"
"Since the Frenchmen have been here
   They have called it Sault-Marie;
But that is a name for priests
   And for not you and me.
It went by another word,"
   Quoth he of the shaven head:

"It was called Ticonderoga
    In the days of the great dead."
And it fell on the morrow's morning,
    In the fiercest of the fight,
That the Cameron bit the dust
    As he foretold at night;
And far from the hills of heather,
    Far from the isles of the sea,
He sleeps in the place of the name
    As it was doomed to be.

HEATHER ALE

A GALLOWAY LEGEND

FROM the bonny bells of heather
   They brewed a drink long-syne,
Was sweeter far than honey,
   Was stronger far than wine.
They brewed it and they drank it,
   And lay in a blessed swound
For days and days together
   In their dwellings underground.

There rose a king in Scotland,
   A fell man to his foes,
He smote the Picts in battle,
   He hunted them like roes.
Over miles of the red mountain
   He hunted as they fled,
And strewed the dwarfish bodies
   Of the dying and the dead.

Summer came in the country,
   Red was the heather bell;
But the manner of the brewing
   None was alive to tell.
In graves that were like children's
   On many a mountain head,
The Brewsters of the Heather
   Lay numbered with the dead.

The king in the red moorland
　　Rode on a summer's day;
And the bees hummed, and the curlews
　　Cried beside the way.
The king rode, and was angry,
　　Black was his brow and pale,
To rule in a land of heather
　　And lack the Heather Ale.

It fortuned that his vassals,
　　Riding free on the heath,
Came on a stone that was fallen
　　And vermin hid beneath.
Rudely plucked from their hiding,
　　Never a word they spoke:
A son and his aged father—
　　Last of the dwarfish folk.

The king sat high on his charger,
　　He looked on the little men;
And the dwarfish and swarthy couple
　　Looked at the king again.
Down by the shore he had them;
　　And there on the giddy brink—
"I will give you life, ye vermin,
　　For the secret of the drink."

There stood the son and father,
　　And they looked high and low;
The heather was red around them,
　　The sea rumbled below.

And up and spoke the father,
 Shrill was his voice to hear:
"I have a word in private,
 A word for the royal ear.

"Life is dear to the aged,
 And honour a little thing;
I would gladly sell the secret,"
 Quoth the Pict to the King.
His voice was small as a sparrow's,
 And shrill and wonderful clear:
"I would gladly sell my secret,
 Only my son I fear.

"For life is a little matter,
 And death is nought to the young;
And I dare not sell my honour
 Under the eye of my son.
Take *him*, O king, and bind him,
 And cast him far in the deep;
And it's I will tell the secret
 That I have sworn to keep."
They took the son and bound him,
 Neck and heels in a thong,
And a lad took him and swung him,
 And flung him far and strong,
And the sea swallowed his body,
 Like that of a child of ten;—
And there on the cliff stood the father,
 Last of the dwarfish men.

"True was the word I told you:
   Only my son I feared;
For I doubt the sapling courage
   That goes without the beard.
But now in vain is the torture,
   Fire shall never avail:
Here dies in my bosom
   The secret of Heather Ale."

CHRISTMAS AT SEA

THE sheets were frozen hard, and they cut the naked
    hand;
The decks were like a slide, where a seaman scarce
    could stand;
The wind was a nor'wester, blowing squally off the
    sea;
And cliffs and spouting breakers were the only things
    a-lee.

They heard the surf a-roaring before the break of
    day;
But 'twas only with the peep of light we saw how ill
    we lay.
We tumbled every hand on deck instanter, with a
    shout,
And we gave her the maintops'l, and stood by to go
    about.

All day we tacked and tacked between the South Head
    and the North;
All day we hauled the frozen sheets, and got no fur-
    ther forth;
All day as cold as charity, in bitter pain and dread,
For very life and nature we tacked from head to head.

We gave the South a wider berth, for there the tide-
    race roared;

But every tack made we brought the North Head
    close aboard:
So 's we saw the cliffs and houses, and the breakers
    running high,
And the coastguard in his garden, with his glass
    against his eye.

The frost was on the village roofs as white as ocean
    foam;
The good red fires were burning bright in every 'long-
    shore home;
The windows sparkled clear, and the chimneys vol-
    leyed out;
And I vow we sniffed the victuals as the vessel went
    about.

The bells upon the church were rung with a mighty
    jovial cheer;
For it's just that I should tell you how (of all days in
    the year)
This day of our adversity was blessèd Christmas
    morn,
And the house above the coastguard's was the house
    where I was born.

O well I saw the pleasant room, the pleasant faces
    there,
My mother's silver spectacles, my father's silver hair;
And well I saw the firelight, like a flight of homely
    elves,
Go dancing round the china-plates that stand upon
    the shelves.

And well I knew the talk they had, the talk that was
of me,
Of the shadow on the household and the son that
went to sea;
And O the wicked fool I seemed, in every kind of way,
To be here and hauling frozen ropes on blessèd
Christmas Day.

They lit the high sea-light, and the dark began to fall.
"All hands to loose topgallant sails," I heard the
captain call.
"By the Lord, she'll never stand it," our first mate,
Jackson, cried.
. . . "It's the one way or the other, Mr. Jackson," he
replied.

She staggered to her bearings, but the sails were
new and good,
And the ship smelt up to windward just as though she
understood.
As the winter's day was ending, in the entry of the
night,
We cleared the weary headland, and passed below the
light.

And they heaved a mighty breath, every soul on board
but me,
As they saw her nose again pointing handsome out
to sea;
But all that I could think of, in the darkness and the
cold,
Was just that I was leaving home and my folks were
growing old.

THE SIRE DE MALÉTROIT'S DOOR

D ENIS DE BEAULIEU was not yet two-and-twenty, but he counted himself a grown man, and a very accomplished cavalier into the bargain. Lads were early formed in that rough, warfaring epoch; and when one has been in a pitched battle and a dozen raids, has killed one's man in an honorable fashion, and knows a thing or two of strategy and mankind, a certain swagger in the gait is surely to be pardoned. He had put up his horse with due care, and supped with due deliberation; and then, in a very agreeable frame of mind, went out to pay a visit in the gray of the evening. It was not a very wise proceeding on the young man's part. He would have done better to remain beside the fire or go decently to bed. For the town was full of the troops of Burgundy and England under a mixed command; and though Denis was there on safe-conduct, his safe-conduct was like to serve him little on a chance encounter.

It was September, 1429; the weather had fallen sharp; a flighty piping wind, laden with showers, beat about the township; and the dead leaves ran riot along the streets. Here and there a window was already lighted up; and the noise of men-at-arms making merry over supper within, came forth in fits and was swallowed up and carried away by the wind.

The night fell swiftly; the flag of England, fluttering on the spire-top, grew ever fainter and fainter against the flying clouds—a black speck like a swallow in the tumultuous, leaden chaos of the sky. As the night fell the wind rose, and began to hoot under archways and roar amid the tree-tops in the valley below the town.

Denis de Beaulieu walked fast and was soon knocking at his friend's door; but though he promised himself to stay only a little while and make an early return, his welcome was so pleasant, and he found so much to delay him, that it was already long past midnight before he said good-bye upon the threshold. The wind had fallen again in the meanwhile; the night was as black as the grave; not a star, nor a glimmer of moonshine, slipped through the canopy of cloud. Denis was ill-acquainted with the intricate lanes of Chateau Landon; even by daylight he had found some trouble in picking his way; and in this absolute darkness he soon lost it altogether. He was certain of one thing only—to keep mounting the hill; for his friend's house lay at the lower end, or tail, of Chateau Landon, while the inn was up at the head, under the great church spire. With this clue to go upon he stumbled and groped forward, now breathing more freely in open places where there was a good slice of sky overhead, now feeling along the wall in stifling closes. It is an eerie and mysterious position to be thus submerged in opaque blackness in an almost unknown town. The silence is terrifying in its possibilities. The touch of cold window

bars to the exploring hand startles the man like the
touch of a toad; the inequalities of the pavement
shake his heart into his mouth; a piece of denser
darkness threatens an ambuscade or a chasm in the
pathway; and where the air is brighter, the houses
put on strange and bewildering appearances, as if to
lead him farther from his way. For Denis, who had
to regain his inn without attracting notice, there was
real danger as well as mere discomfort in the walk;
and he went warily and boldly at once, and at every
corner paused to make an observation.

He had been for some time threading a lane so
narrow that he could touch a wall with either hand
when it began to open out and go sharply downward.
Plainly this lay no longer in the direction of his inn;
but the hope of a little more light tempted him for-
ward to reconnoitre. The lane ended in a terrace
with a bartizan wall, which gave an outlook between
high houses, as out of an embrasure, into the valley
lying dark and formless several hundred feet below.
Denis looked down, and could discern a few tree-tops
waving and a single speck of brightness where the
river ran across a weir. The weather was clearing
up, and the sky had lightened, so as to show the out-
line of the heavier clouds and the dark margin of the
hills. By the uncertain glimmer, the house on his
left hand should be a place of some pretensions; it
was surmounted by several pinnacles and turret-tops;
the round stern of a chapel, with a fringe of flying
buttresses, projected boldly from the main block;
and the door was sheltered under a deep porch

carved with figures and overhung by two long gargoyles. The windows of the chapel gleamed through their intricate tracery with a light as of many tapers, and threw out the buttresses and the peaked roof in a more intense blackness against the sky. It was plainly the hotel of some great family of the neighborhood; and as it reminded Denis of a town house of his own at Bourges, he stood for some time gazing up at it and mentally gauging the skill of the architects and the consideration of the two families.

There seemed to be no issue to the terrace but the lane by which he had reached it; he could only retrace his steps, but he gained some notion of his whereabouts, and hoped by this means to hit the main thoroughfare and speedily regain the inn. He was reckoning without that chapter of accidents which was to make this night memorable above all others in his career; for he had not gone back above a hundred yards before he saw a light coming to meet him, and heard loud voices speaking together in the echoing narrows of the lane. It was a party of men-at-arms going the night round with torches. Denis assured himself that they had all been making free with the wine-bowl, and were in no mood to be particular about safe-conducts or the niceties of chivalrous war. It was as like as not that they would kill him like a dog and leave him where he fell. The situation was inspiriting but nervous. Their own torches would conceal him from sight, he reflected; and he hoped that they would drown the noise of his footsteps with their own empty voices. If he were but fleet and silent, he might evade their notice altogether.

Unfortunately, as he turned to beat a retreat, his foot rolled upon a pebble; he fell against the wall with an ejaculation, and his sword rang loudly on the stones. Two or three voices demanded who went there—some in French, some in English; but Denis made no reply, and ran the faster down the lane. Once upon the terrace, he paused to look back. They still kept calling after him, and just then began to double the pace in pursuit, with a considerable clank of armor, and great tossing of the torchlight to and fro in the narrow jaws of the passage.

Denis cast a look around and darted into the porch. There he might escape observation, or—if that were too much to expect—was in a capital posture whether for parley or defence. So thinking, he drew his sword and tried to set his back against the door. To his surprise, it yielded behind his weight; and though he turned in a moment, continued to swing back on oiled and noiseless hinges, until it stood wide open on a black interior. When things fall out opportunely for the person concerned, he is not apt to be critical about the how or why, his own immediate personal convenience seeming a sufficient reason for the strangest oddities and revolutions in our sublunary things; and so Denis, without a moment's hesitation, stepped within and partly closed the door behind him to conceal his place of refuge. Nothing was further from his thoughts than to close it altogether; but for some inexplicable reason—perhaps by a spring or a weight

—the ponderous mass of oak whipped itself out of his fingers and clanked to, with a formidable rumble and a noise like the falling of an automatic bar.

The round, at that very moment, debouched upon the terrace and proceeded to summon him with shouts and curses. He heard them ferreting in the dark corners; the stock of a lance even rattled along the outer surface of the door behind which he stood; but these gentlemen were in too high a humor to be long delayed, and soon made off down a corkscrew pathway which had escaped Denis's observation, and passed out of sight and hearing along the battlements of the town.

Denis breathed again. He gave them a few minutes' grace for fear of accidents, and then groped about for some means of opening the door and slipping forth again. The inner surface was quite smooth, not a handle, not a moulding, not a projection of any sort. He got his finger-nails round the edges and pulled, but the mass was immovable. He shook it, it was as firm as a rock. Denis de Beaulieu frowned and gave vent to a little noiseless whistle. What ailed the door? he wondered. Why was it open? How came it to shut so easily and so effectually after him? There was something obscure and underhand about all this, that was little to the young man's fancy. It looked like a snare, and yet who could suppose a snare in such a quiet by-street, and in a house of so prosperous and even noble an exterior? And yet—snare or no snare, intentionally or unintentionally—here he was, prettily trapped;

and for the life of him he could see no way out of it
again. The darkness began to weigh upon him. He
gave ear; all was silent without, but within and close
by he seemed to catch a faint sighing, a faint sobbing
rustle, a little stealthy creak—as though many per-
sons were at his side, holding themselves quite still,
and governing even their respiration with the extreme
of slyness. The idea went to his vitals with a shock,
and he faced about suddenly as if to defend his life.
Then, for the first time, he became aware of a light
about the level of his eyes and at some distance in
the interior of the house—a vertical thread of light,
widening towards the bottom, such as might escape
between two wings of arras over a doorway. To see
anything was a relief to Denis; it was like a piece of
solid ground to a man laboring in a morass; his mind
seized upon it with avidity; and he stood staring at
it and trying to piece together some logical concep-
tion of his surroundings. Plainly there was a flight
of steps ascending from his own level to that of this
illuminated doorway; and indeed he thought he could
make out another thread of light, as fine as a needle,
and as faint as phosphorescence, which might very
well be reflected along the polished wood of a hand-
rail. Since he had begun to suspect that he was not
alone, his heart had continued to beat with smother-
ing violence, and an intolerable desire for action of
any sort had possessed itself of his spirit. He was in
deadly peril, he believed. What could be more natu-
ral than to mount the staircase, lift the curtain, and
confront his difficulty at once? At least he would

be dealing with something tangible; at least he would be no longer in the dark. He stepped slowly forward with outstretched hands, until his foot struck the bottom step; then he rapidly scaled the stairs, stood for a moment to compose his expression, lifted the arras and went in.

He found himself in a large apartment of polished stone. There were three doors; one on each of three sides; all similarly curtained with tapestry. The fourth side was occupied by two large windows and a great stone chimneypiece, carved with the arms of the Malétroits. Denis recognized the bearings, and was gratified to find himself in such good hands. The room was strongly illuminated; but it contained little furniture except a heavy table and a chair or two, the hearth was innocent of fire, and the pavement was but sparsely strewn with rushes clearly many days old.

On a high chair beside the chimney, and directly facing Denis as he entered, sat a little old gentleman in a fur tippet. He sat with his legs crossed and his hands folded, and a cup of spiced wine stood by his elbow on a bracket on the wall. His countenance had a strongly masculine cast; not properly human, but such as we see in the bull, the goat, or the domestic boar; something equivocal and wheedling, something greedy, brutal, and dangerous. The upper lip was inordinately full, as though swollen by a blow or a toothache; and the smile, the peaked eyebrows, and the small, strong eyes were quaintly and almost comically evil in expression. Beautiful white hair hung straight all round his head, like a saint's, and fell in a single curl upon the tippet. His beard and moustache were the pink of venerable sweetness. Age, probably in consequence of inordinate precautions, had left no mark upon his hands; and the Malétroit hand was famous. It would be difficult to imagine anything at once so fleshy and so delicate in design; the taper, sensual fingers, were like those of one of Leonardo's women; the fork of the thumb made a dimpled protuberance when closed; the nails were perfectly shaped, and of a dead, surprising whiteness. It rendered his aspect tenfold more redoubtable, that a man with hands like these should keep them devoutly folded like a virgin martyr—that a man with so intent and startling an expression of face should sit patiently on his seat and contemplate people with an unwinking stare, like a god, or a god's statue. His quiescence seemed ironical and treacherous, it fitted so poorly with his looks.

Such was Alain, Sire de Malétroit.

Denis and he looked silently at each other for a second or two.

"Pray step in," said the Sire de Malétroit. "I have been expecting you all the evening."

He had not risen but he accompanied his words with a smile and a slight but courteous inclination of the head. Partly from the smile, partly from the strange musical murmur with which the Sire prefaced his observation, Denis felt a strong shudder of disgust go through his marrow. And what with disgust and honest confusion of mind, he could scarcely get words together in reply.

"I fear," he said, "that this is a double accident. I am not the person you suppose me. It seems you were looking for a visit; but for my part, nothing was further from my thoughts—nothing could be more contrary to my wishes—than this intrusion."

"Well, well," replied the old gentleman indulgently, "here you are, which is the main point. Seat yourself, my friend, and put yourself entirely at your ease. We shall arrange our little affairs presently."

Denis perceived that the matter was still complicated with some misconception, and he hastened to continue his explanations.

"Your door . . . " he began.

"About my door?" asked the other raising his peaked eyebrows. "A little piece of ingenuity." He shrugged his shoulders. "A hospitable fancy! By your own account, you were not desirous of making my acquaintance. We old people look for such reluctance now and then; when it touches our honor, we cast about until we find some way of overcoming it. You arrive uninvited, but believe me, very welcome."

"You persist in error, sir," said Denis. "There can be no question between you and me. I am a stranger in this countryside. My name is Denis, damoiseau de Beaulieu. If you see me in your house, it is only——"

"My young friend," interrupted the other, "you

will permit me to have my own ideas on that subject. They probably differ from yours at the present moment," he added with a leer, "but time will show which of us is in the right."

Denis was convinced he had to do with a lunatic. He seated himself with a shrug, content to wait the upshot; and a pause ensued, during which he thought he could distinguish a hurried gabbling as of prayer from behind the arras immediately opposite him. Sometimes there seemed to be but one person engaged, sometimes two; and the vehemence of the voice, low as it was, seemed to indicate either great haste or an agony of spirit. It occurred to him that this piece of tapestry covered the entrance to the chapel he had noticed from without.

The old gentleman meanwhile surveyed Denis from head to foot with a smile, and from time to time emitted little noises like a bird or a mouse, which seemed to indicate a high degree of satisfaction. This state of matters became rapidly insupportable; and Denis, to put an end to it, remarked politely that the wind had gone down.

The old gentleman fell into a fit of silent laughter, so prolonged and violent that he became quite red in the face. Denis got upon his feet at once, and put on his hat with a flourish.

"Sir," he said, "if you are in your wits, you have affronted me grossly. If you are out of them, I flatter myself I can find better employment for my brains than to talk with lunatics. My conscience is clear; you have made a fool of me from the first moment;

you have refused to hear my explanations; and now there is no power under God will make me stay here any longer; and if I cannot make my way out in a more decent fashion, I will hack your door in pieces with my sword."

The Sire de Malétroit raised his right hand and wagged it at Denis with the fore and little fingers extended.

"My dear nephew," he said, "sit down."

"Nephew!" retorted Denis, "you lie in your throat;" and he snapped his fingers in his face.

"Sit down, you rogue!" cried the old gentleman, in a sudden, harsh voice, like the barking of a dog. "Do you fancy," he went on, "that when I had made my little contrivance for the door I had stopped short with that? If you prefer to be bound hand and foot till your bones ache, rise and try to go away. If you choose to remain a free young buck, agreeably conversing with an old gentleman—why, sit where you are in peace, and God be with you."

"Do you mean I am a prisoner?" demanded Denis.

"I state the facts," replied the other. "I would rather leave the conclusion to yourself."

Denis sat down again. Externally he managed to keep pretty calm, but within, he was now boiling with anger, now chilled with apprehension. He no longer felt convinced that he was dealing with a madman. And if the old gentleman was sane, what, in God's name, had he to look for? What absurd or tragical adventure had befallen him? What countenance was he to assume?

While he was thus unpleasantly reflecting, the arras that overhung the chapel door was raised, and a tall priest in his robes came forth and, giving a long, keen stare at Denis said something in an undertone to Sire de Malétroit.

"She is in a better frame of spirit?" asked the latter.

"She is more resigned, messire," replied the priest.

"Now the Lord help her, she is hard to please!" sneered the old gentleman. "A likely stripling—not ill-born—and of her own choosing, too? Why, what more would the jade have?"

"The situation is not usual for a young damsel," said the other, "and somewhat trying to her blushes."

"She should have thought of that before she began the dance. It was none of my choosing, God knows that: but since she is in it, by our lady, she shall carry it to the end." And then addressing Denis, "Monsieur de Beaulieu," he asked, "may I present you to my niece? She has been waiting your arrival, I may say, with even greater impatience than myself."

Denis had resigned himself with a good grace—all he desired was to know the worst of it as speedily as possible; so he rose at once, and bowed in acquiescence. The Sire de Malétroit followed his example and limped, with the assistance of the chaplain's arm, towards the chapel-door. The priest pulled aside the arras, and all three entered. The building had considerable architectural pretensions. A light groining sprang from six stout columns, and hung down in two rich pendants from the centre of the vault. The place terminated behind the altar in a round end, embossed and honeycombed with a superfluity of ornament in relief, and pierced by many little windows shaped like stars, trefoils, or wheels. These windows were imperfectly glazed, so that the night air circulated freely in the chapel. The tapers, of which there must have been half a hundred burning on the altar, were unmercifully blown about; and the light went through many different phases of brilliancy and semi-eclipse. On the steps in front of the altar knelt a young girl richly attired as a bride. A chill settled over Denis as he observed her costume; he fought with desperate energy against the conclusion that was being thrust upon his mind; it could not— it should not—be as he feared.

"Blanche," said the Sire, in his most flute-like tones, "I have brought a friend to see you, my little girl; turn round and give him your pretty hand. It is good to be devout; but it is necessary to be polite, my niece."

The girl rose to her feet and turned toward the new comers. She moved all of a piece; and shame and exhaustion were expressed in every line of her fresh young body; and she held her head down and kept her eyes upon the pavement, as she came slowly forward. In the course of her advance, her eyes fell upon Denis de Beaulieu's feet—feet of which he was justly vain, be it remarked, and wore in the most elegant accoutrement even while traveling. She paused —started, as if his yellow boots had conveyed some shocking meaning—and glanced suddenly up into the wearer's countenance. Their eyes met; shame gave place to horror and terror in her looks; the blood left her lips; with a piercing scream she covered her face with her hands and sank upon the chapel floor.

"That is not the man!" she cried. "My uncle, that is not the man!"

The Sire de Malétroit chirped agreeably. "Of course not," he said, "I expected as much. It was so unfortunate you could not remember his name."

"Indeed," she cried, "indeed, I have never seen this person till this moment—I have never so much as set eyes upon him—I never wish to see him again. Sir," she said, turning to Denis, "if you are a gentleman, you will bear me out. Have I ever seen you—have you ever seen me—before this accursed hour?"

"To speak for myself, I have never had that pleasure," answered the young man. "This is the first time, messire, that I have met with your engaging niece."

The old gentleman shrugged his shoulders.

"I am distressed to hear it," he said. "But it is never too late to begin. I had little more acquaintance with my own late lady ere I married her; which proves," he added, with a grimace, "that these impromptu marriages may often produce an excellent understanding in the long run. As the bridegroom is to have a voice in the matter, I will give him two hours to make up for lost time before we proceed with the ceremony." And he turned toward the door, followed by the clergyman.

The girl was on her feet in a moment. "My uncle,

you cannot be in earnest," she said. "I declare before God I will stab myself rather than be forced on that young man. The heart rises at it; God forbids such marriages; you dishonor your white hair. Oh, my uncle, pity me! There is not a woman in all the world but would prefer death to such a nuptial. Is it possible," she added, faltering—"is it possible that you do not believe me—that you still think this"—and she pointed at Denis with a tremor of anger and contempt—"that you still think *this* to be the man?"

"Frankly," said the old gentleman, pausing on the threshold, "I do. But let me explain to you once for all, Blanche de Malétroit, my way of thinking about this affair. When you took it into your head to dishonor my family and the name that I have borne, in peace and war, for more than three-score years, you forfeited, not only the right to question my designs, but that of looking me in the face. If your father had been alive, he would have spat on you and turned you out of doors. His was the hand of iron. You may bless your God you have only to deal with the hand of velvet, mademoiselle. It was my duty to get you married without delay. Out of pure good-will, I have tried to find your own gallant for you. And I believe I have succeeded. But before God and all the holy angels, Blanche de Malétroit, if I have not, I care not one jack-straw. So let me recommend you to be polite to our young friend; for upon my word, your next groom may be less appetizing."

And with that he went out, with the chaplain at his heels; and the arras fell behind the pair.

The girl turned upon Denis with flashing eyes.

"And what, sir," she demanded, "may be the meaning of all this?"

"God knows," returned Denis, gloomily. "I am a prisoner in this house, which seems full of mad people. More I know not; and nothing do I understand."

"And pray how came you here," she asked.

He told her as briefly as he could. "For the rest," he added, "perhaps you will follow my example, and tell me the answer to all these riddles, and what, in God's name, is like to be the end of it."

She stood silent for a little, and he could see her lips tremble and her tearless eyes burn with a feverish lustre. Then she pressed her forehead in both hands.

"Alas, how my head aches!" she said wearily—"to say nothing of my poor heart! But it is due to you to know my story, unmaidenly as it must seem. I am called Blanche de Malétroit; I have been without father or mother for—oh! for as long as I can recollect, and indeed I have been most unhappy all my life. Three months ago a young captain began to stand near me every day in church. I could see that I pleased him; I am much to blame, but I was so glad that anyone should love me; and when he passed me a letter, I took it home with me and read it with great pleasure. Since that time he has written many. He was so anxious to speak with me, poor fellow! and kept asking me to leave the door open some evening that we might have two words upon the stair. For he knew how much my uncle trusted me." She gave something like a sob at that, and it was a moment before she could go on. "My uncle is a hard man, but he is very shrewd," she said at last. "He has performed many feats in war, and was a great person at court, and much trusted by Queen Isabeau in old days. How he came to suspect me I cannot tell; but it is hard to keep anything from his knowledge; and this morning, as we came from mass, he took my hand into his, forced it open, and read my little billet, walking by my side all the while. When he finished, he gave it back to me with great politeness. It contained another request to have the door left open; and this has been the ruin of us all. My uncle kept me strictly in my roon until evening, and then ordered me to dress myself as you see me—a hard mockery for a young girl, do you not think so? I suppose, when he could not prevail with me to tell him the young captain's name, he must have laid a trap for him: into which, alas! you have fallen in the anger of God. I looked for much confusion; for how could I tell whether he was willing to take me for his wife on these sharp terms? He might have been trifling with me from the first; or I might have made myself too cheap in his eyes. But truly I had not looked for such a shameful punishment as this! I could not think that God would let a girl be so disgraced before a young man. And now I tell you all; and I can scarcely hope that you will not despise me."

Denis made her a respectful inclination.

"Madam," he said, "you have honored me by your

confidence. It remains for me to prove that I am
not unworthy of the honor. Is Messire de Malétroit
at hand?"

"I believe he is writing in the salle without," she
answered.

"May I lead you thither, madam?" asked Denis,
offering his hand with his most courtly bearing.

She accepted it; and the pair passed out of the
chapel, Blanche in a very drooping and shamefaced
condition, but Denis strutting and ruffling in the con-
sciousness of a mission, and the boyish certainty of
accomplishing it with honor.

The Sire de Malétroit rose to meet them with an
ironical obeisance.

"Sir," said Denis, with the grandest possible air,
"I believe I am to have some say in the matter of this
marriage; and let me tell you at once, I will be no
party to forcing the inclination of this young lady.
Had it been freely offered to me, I should have been
proud to accept her hand, for I perceive she is as
good as she is beautiful; but as things are, I have
now the honor, messire, of refusing."

Blanche looked at him with gratitude in her eyes;
but the old gentleman only smiled and smiled, until
his smile grew positively sickening to Denis.

"I am afraid," he said, "Monsieur de Beaulieu,
that you do not perfectly understand the choice I
have offered you. Follow me, I beseech you, to this
window." And he led the way to one of the large
windows which stood open on the night. "You
observe," he went on, "there is an iron ring in the

upper masonry, and reeved through that, a very efficacious rope. Now, mark my words: if you should find your disinclination to my niece's person insurmountable, I shall have you hanged out of this window before sunrise. I shall only proceed to such an extremity with the greatest regret, you may believe me. For it is not at all your death that I desire, but my niece's establishment in life. At the same time, it must come to that if you prove obstinate. Your family, Monsieur de Beaulieu, is very well in its way; but if you sprang from Charlemagne, you should not refuse the hand of a Malétroit with impunity—not if she had been as common as the Paris road—not if she were as hideous as the gargoyle over my door. Neither my niece nor you, nor my own private feelings, move me at all in this matter. The honor of my house has been compromised; I believe you to be the guilty person, at least you are now in the secret; and you can hardly wonder if I request you to wipe out the stain. If you will not, your blood be on your own head! It will be no great satisfaction to me to have your interesting relics kicking their heels in the breeze below my windows, but half a loaf is better than no bread, and if I cannot cure the dishonor, I shall at least stop the scandal."

There was a pause.

"I believe there are other ways of settling such imbroglios among gentlemen," said Denis. "You wear a sword, and I hear you have used it with distinction."

The Sire de Malétroit made a signal to the chaplain, who crossed the room with long silent strides and raised the arras over the third of the three doors. It was only a moment before he let it fall again; but Denis had time to see a dusky passage full of armed men.

"When I was a little younger, I should have been delighted to honor you, Monsieur de Beaulieu," said Sire Alain; "but I am now too old. Faithful retainers are the sinews of age, and I must employ the strength I have. This is one of the hardest things to swallow as a man grows up in years; but with a little patience, even this becomes habitual. You and the lady seem to prefer the salle for what remains of your two hours; and as I have no desire to cross your preference, I shall resign it to your use with all the pleasure in the world. No haste!" he added, holding up his hand, as he saw a dangerous look come into Denis de Beaulieu's face. "If your mind revolt against hanging, it will be time enough two hours hence to throw yourself out of the window or upon the pikes of my retainers. Two hours of life are always two hours. A great many things may turn up in even as little a while as that. And, besides, if I understand her appearance, my niece has something to say to you. You will not disfigure your last hours by a want of politeness to a lady?"

Denis looked at Blanche, and she made him an imploring gesture.

It is likely that the old gentleman was hugely pleased at this symptom of an understanding; for he smiled on both, and added sweetly: "If you will give me your word of honor, Monsieur de Beaulieu, to await my return at the end of the two hours before attempting anything desperate, I shall withdraw my retainers, and let you speak in greater privacy with mademoiselle."

Denis again glanced at the girl, who seemed to beseech him to agree.

"I give you my word of honor," he said.

Messire de Malétroit bowed, and proceeded to limp about the apartment, clearing his throat the while with that odd musical chirp which had already grown so irritating in the ears of Denis de Beaulieu. He first possessed himself of some papers which lay upon the table; then he went to the mouth of the passage and appeared to give an order to the men behind the arras; and lastly he hobbled out through the door by which Denis had come in, turning upon the threshold to address a last smiling bow to the young couple, and followed by the chaplain with a hand-lamp.

No sooner were they alone than Blanche advanced towards Denis with her hands extended. Her face was flushed and excited, and her eyes shone with tears.

"You shall not die!" she cried, "you shall marry me after all."

"You seem to think, madam," replied Denis, "that I stand much in fear of death."

"Oh, no, no," she said, "I see you are no poltroon. It is for my own sake—I could not bear to have you slain for such a scruple."

"I am afraid," returned Denis, "that you underrate the difficulty, madam. What you may be too generous to refuse, I may be too proud to accept. In a moment of noble feeling towards me, you forget what you perhaps owe to others."

He had the decency to keep his eyes on the floor as he said this, and after he had finished, so as not to spy upon her confusion. She stood silent for a moment, then walked suddenly away, and falling on her uncle's chair, fairly burst out sobbing. Denis was in the acme of embarrassment. He looked round, as if to seek for inspiration, and seeing a stool, plumped down upon it for something to do. There he sat playing with the guard of his rapier, and wishing himself dead a thousand times over, and buried in the nastiest kitchen-heap in France. His eyes wandered round the apartment, but found nothing to arrest them. There were such wide spaces between the furniture, the light fell so badly and cheerlessly over all, the dark outside air looked in so coldly through the windows, that he thought he had never seen a church so vast, nor a tomb so melancholy. The regular sobs of Blanche de Malétroit measured out the time like the ticking of a clock. He read the device upon the shield over and over again, until his eyes became obscured; he stared into shadowy corners until he imagined they were swarming with horrible animals; and every now and again he awoke with a start, to remember that his last two hours were running, and death was on the march.

Oftener and oftener, as the time went on, did his glance settle on the girl herself. Her face was bowed forward and covered with her hands, and she was

shaken at intervals by the convulsive hiccup of grief.
Even thus she was not an unpleasant object to dwell
upon, so plump and yet so fine, with a warm brown
skin, and the most beautiful hair, Denis thought, in
the whole world of womankind. Her hands were like
her uncle's: but they were more in place at the end of
her young arms, and looked infinitely soft and caress-
ing. He remembered how her blue eyes had shone
upon him, full of anger, pity, and innocence. And the
more he dwelt on her perfections, the uglier death
looked, and the more deeply was he smitten with
penitence at her continued tears. Now he felt that
no man could have the courage to leave a world which
contained so beautiful a creature; and now he would
have given forty minutes of his last hour to have un-
said his cruel speech.

Suddenly a hoarse and ragged peal of cockcrow
rose to their ears from the dark valley below the win-
dows. And this shattering noise in the silence of all
around was like a light in a dark place, and shook
them both out of their reflections.

"Alas, can I do nothing to help you?" she said,
looking up.

"Madam," replied Denis, with a fine irrelevancy,
"if I have said anything to wound you, believe me, it
was for your own sake and not for mine."

She thanked him with a tearful look.

"I feel your position cruelly," he went on. "The
world has been bitter hard on you. Your uncle is a
disgrace to mankind. Believe me, madam, there is
no young gentleman in all France but would be glad

of my opportunity, to die in doing you a momentary service."

"I know already that you can be very brave and generous," she answered. "What I *want* to know is whether I can serve you—now or afterwards," she added, with a quaver.

"Most certainly," he answered with a smile. "Let me sit beside you as if I were a friend, instead of a foolish intruder; try to forget how awkardly we are placed to one another; make my last moments go pleasantly; and you will do me the chief service possible."

"You are very gallant," she added, with a yet deeper sadness . . . "very gallant . . . and it somehow pains me. But draw nearer, if you please; and if you find anything to say to me, you will at least make certain of a very friendly listener. Ah! Monsieur de Beaulieu," she broke forth—"ah! Monsieur de Beaulieu, how can I look you in the face?" And she fell to weeping again with a renewed effusion.

"Madam," said Denis, taking her hand in both of his, "reflect on the little time I have before me, and the great bitterness into which I am cast by the sight of your distress. Spare me, in my last moments, the spectacle of what I cannot cure even with the sacrifice of my life."

"I am very selfish," answered Blanche. "I will be braver, Monsieur de Beaulieu, for your sake. But think if I can do you no kindness in the future—if you have no friends to whom I could carry your adieux. Charge me as heavily as you can; every burden will lighten, by so little, the invaluable gratitude I owe you. Put it in my power to do something more for you than weep."

"My mother is married again, and has a young family to care for. My brother Guichard will inherit my fiefs; and if I am not in error, that will content him amply for my death. Life is a little vapor that passeth away, as we are told by those in holy orders. When a man is in a fair way and sees all life open in front of him, he seems to himself to make a very important figure in the world. His horse whinnies to him; the trumpets blow and the girls look out of window as he rides into town before his company; he receives many assurances of trust and regard—sometimes by express in a letter—sometimes face to face, with persons of great consequence falling on his neck. It is not wonderful if his head is turned for a time. But once he is dead, were he as brave as Hercules or as wise as Solomon, he is soon forgotten. It is not ten years since my father fell, with many other knights around him, in a very fierce encounter, and I do not think that any one of them, nor so much as the name of the fight, is now remembered. No, no, madam, the nearer you come to it, you see that death is a dark and dusty corner, where a man gets into his tomb and has the door shut after him till the judgment day. I have few friends just now, and once I am dead I shall have none."

"Ah, Monsieur de Beaulieu!" she exclaimed, "you forget Blanche de Malétroit."

"You have a sweet nature, madam, and you are pleased to estimate a little service far beyond its worth."

"It is not that," she answered. "You mistake me if you think I am easily touched by my own concerns. I say so, because you are the noblest man I have ever met; because I recognize in you a spirit that would have made even a common person famous in the land."

"And yet here I die in a mousetrap—with no more noise about it than my own squeaking," answered he.

A look of pain crossed her face, and she was silent for a little while. Then a light came into her eyes, and with a smile she spoke again.

"I cannot have my champion think meanly of himself. Anyone who gives his life for another will be met in Paradise by all the heralds and angels of the Lord God. And you have no such cause to hang your head. For . . . Pray, do you think me beautiful?" she asked, with a deep flush.

"Indeed, madam, I do," he said.

"I am glad of that," she answered heartily. "Do you think there are many men in France who have been asked in marriage by a beautiful maiden—with her own lips—and who have refused her to her face? I know you men would half despise such a triumph; but believe me, we women know more of what is precious in love. There is nothing that should set a person higher in his own esteem; and we women would prize nothing more dearly."

"You are very good," he said; "but you cannot make me forget that I was asked in pity and not for love."

"I am not so sure of that," she replied, holding down her head. "Hear me to an end, Monsieur de Beaulieu. I know how you must despise me; I feel you are right to do so; I am too poor a creature to occupy one thought of your mind, although, alas! you must die for me this morning. But when I asked you to marry me, indeed, and indeed, it was because I respected and admired you, and loved you with my whole soul, from the very moment that you took my part against my uncle. If you had seen yourself, and how noble you looked, you would pity rather than despise me. And now," she went on, hurriedly checking him with her hand, "although I have laid aside all reserve and told you so much, remember that I know your sentiments towards me already. I would not, believe me, being nobly born, weary you with importunities into consent. I too have a pride of my own; and I declare before the holy mother of God, if you should now go back from your word already given, I would no more marry you than I would marry my uncle's groom."

Denis smiled a little bitterly.

"It is a small love," he said, "that shies at a little pride."

She made no answer, although she probably had her own thoughts.

"Come hither to the window," he said with a sigh. "Here is the dawn."

And indeed the dawn was already beginning. The hollow of the sky was full of essential daylight, colorless and clean; and the valley underneath was flooded with a gray reflection. A few thin vapors clung in the coves of the forest or lay along the winding course of the river. The scene disengaged a surprising effect of stillness, which was hardly interrupted when the cocks began once more to crow among the steadings. Perhaps the same fellow who had made so horrid a clangor in the darkness not half an hour before, now sent up the merriest cheer to greet the coming day. A little wind went bustling and eddying among the tree-tops underneath the windows. And still the daylight kept flooding insensibly out of the east, which was soon to grow incandescent and cast up that red-hot cannon-ball, the rising sun.

Denis looked out over all this with a bit of a shiver. He had taken her hand, and retained it in his almost unconsciously.

"Has the day begun already?" she said; and then, illogically enough: "the night has been so long! Alas! what shall we say to my uncle when he returns?"

"What you will," said Denis, and he pressed her fingers in his.

She was silent.

"Blanche," he said, with a swift, uncertain, passionate utterance, "you have seen whether I fear death. You must know well enough that I would as gladly leap out of that window into the empty air as to lay a finger on you without your free and full consent. But if you care for me at all do not let me lose my life in a misapprehension; for I love you better than the whole world; and though I will die for you blithely, it would be like all the joys of Paradise to live on and spend my life in your service."

As he stopped speaking, a bell began to ring loudly in the interior of the house; and a clatter of armor in the corridor showed that the retainers were returning to their post, and the two hours were at an end.

"After all that you have heard?" she whispered, leaning towards him with her lips and eyes.

"I have heard nothing," he replied.

"The captain's name was Florimond de Champdivers," she said in his ear.

"I did not hear it," he answered, taking her supple body in his arms, and covered her wet face with kisses.

A melodious chirping was audible behind, followed by a beautiful chuckle, and the voice of Messire de Malétroit wished his new nephew a good morning.

THE BOTTLE IMP

I

THERE was a man of the Island of Hawaii whom I shall call Keawe; for the truth is, he still lives and his name must be kept secret; but the place of his birth was not far from Honaunau, where the bones of Keawe the Great lie hidden in a cave. This man was poor, brave, and active; he could read and write like a school-master; he was a first-rate mariner besides, sailed for some time in the island steamers, and steered a whale-boat on the Hamakua coast. At length it came in Keawe's mind to have a sight of the great world and foreign cities, and he shipped on a vessel bound to San Francisco.

This is a fine town, with a fine harbor and a rich people uncountable, and in particular there is one hill which is covered with palaces. Upon this hill Keawe was one day taking a walk, with his pocket full of money, viewing the great houses upon either hand with pleasure.

"What fine houses these are!" he was thinking, "and how happy must these people be who dwell in them and take no care for the morrow."

The thought was in his mind when he came abreast of a house that was smaller than some others, but all finished and beautiful like a toy; the steps of that house shone like silver, and the borders of the garden bloomed like garlands; and the windows were bright like diamonds; and Keawe stopped and wondered at the excellence of all he saw. So, stopping, he was aware of a man that looked forth upon him through a window so clear that Keawe could see him as you see a fish in a pool upon the reef. The man was elderly, with a bald head and a black beard; and his face was heavy with sorrow, and he bitterly sighed. And the truth of it is that as Keawe looked in upon the man, and the man looked out upon Keawe, each envied the other.

All of a sudden the man smiled and nodded, and beckoned Keawe to enter, and met him in the door of the house.

"This is a fine house of mine," said the man, and bitterly sighed. "Would you not care to view the chambers?"

So he led Keawe all over it from the cellar to the roof, and there was nothing there that was not perfect of its kind, and Keawe was astonished.

"Truly," said Keawe, "this is a beautiful house. If I lived in the like of it, I should be laughing all day long; how comes it, then, that you should be sighing?"

"There is no reason," said the man, "why you should not have a house similar to this, and finer, if you wish. You have some money, I suppose?"

"I have fifty dollars," said Keawe, "but a house like this will cost more than fifty dollars."

The man made a computation.

"I am sorry you have no more," said he, "for it may raise you trouble in the future; but it shall be yours at fifty dollars."

"The house?" asked Keawe.

"No, not the house," replied the man, "but the bottle. For I must tell you, although I appear to you so rich and fortunate, all my fortune, and this house itself and its garden, came out of a bottle not much bigger than a pint. This is it."

And he opened a lock-fast place and he took out a round-bellied bottle with a long neck. The glass of it was white, like milk, with changing rainbow colors in the grain; while inside something obscurely moved, like a shadow and a fire.

"This is the bottle," said the man; and when Keawe laughed, "You do not believe me?" he added. "Try, then, for yourself. See if you can break it."

So Keawe took the bottle up and dashed it on the floor till he was weary, but it jumped on the floor, like a child's ball, and was not injured.

"This is a strange thing," said Keawe; "for by the touch of it, as well as by the look, the bottle should be of glass."

"Of glass it is," replied the man, sighing more heavily than ever; "but the glass of it was tempered in the flames of hell. An imp lives in it, and that is the shadow we behold there moving; or so I suppose. If any man buys this bottle, the imp is at his command; all that he desires: love, fame, money, houses like this house—ay, or a city like this city—all are his at the word uttered. Napoleon had this bottle, and by it he grew to be the king of the world, but he sold it at the last and fell. Captain Cook had this bottle, and by it found his way to so many islands; but he, too, sold it, and was slain upon Hawaii. For once it is sold, the power goes, and the protection; and unless a man remain content with what he has, ill will befall him."

"And yet you talk of selling it yourself?" Keawe said.

"I have all I wish, and I am growing elderly," replied the man. "There is one thing the imp can not do; he can not prolong life; and it would not be fair to conceal from you there is a drawback to the bottle, for if a man dies before he sells it he must burn in hell forever."

"To be sure, that is a drawback, and no mistake," cried Keawe. "I would not meddle with the thing. I can do without a house, thank God! but there is one thing I could not be doing with one particle, and that is to be damned."

"Dear me! you must not run away with things," returned the man. "All you have to do is to use the power of the imp in moderation, and then sell it to some one else, as I do to you, and finish your life in comfort."

"Well, I observe two things," said Keawe. "All the time you keep sighing like a maid in love; that is one. And for the other you sell this bottle very cheap."

"I have told you already why I sigh," said the man. "It is because I fear my health is breaking up; and, as you said yourself, to die and go to the devil is a pity for any one. As for why I sell so cheap, I must explain to you there is a peculiarity about the bottle. Long ago, when the devil brought it first upon the earth, it was extremely expensive, and was sold first of all to Prester John for many millions of dollars; but it can not be sold at all, unless sold at a loss. If you sell it for as much as you paid for it, back it comes to you again, like a homing pigeon. It follows that the price has kept falling in these centuries, and the bottle is now remarkably cheap. I bought it myself from one of my great neighbors on this hill, and the price I paid was only ninety dollars. I could sell it for as high as eighty-nine dollars and ninety-nine cents, but not a penny dearer, or back the thing must come to me. Now, about this there are two bothers. First, when you offer a bottle so singular for eighty-odd dollars, people suppose you to be jesting. And second—but there is no hurry about that, and I need not go into it. Only remember, it must be coined money that you sell it for."

"How am I to know that this is all true?" asked Keawe.

"Some of it you can try at once," replied the man. "Give me your fifty dollars, take the bottle, and wish your fifty dollars back into your pocket. If that does not happen, I pledge you my honor I will cry off the bargain and restore your money."

"You are not deceiving me?" said Keawe.

The man bound himself with a great oath.

"Well, I will risk that much," said Keawe, "for that can do no harm."

And he paid over his money to the man, and the man handed him the bottle.

"Imp of the bottle," said Keawe, "I want my fifty dollars back."

And, sure enough, he had scarce said the word before his pocket was as heavy as ever.

"To be sure, this is a wonderful bottle!" said Keawe.

"And now, good-morning to you, my fine fellow, and the devil go with you for me!" said the man.

"Hold on!" said Keawe; "I don't want any more of this fun. Here, take your bottle back."

"You have bought it for less than I paid for it," replied the man, rubbing his hands. "It is yours now, and for my part, I am only concerned to see the back of you."

And with that he rang for his Chinese servant and had Keawe shown out of the house.

Now, when Keawe was in the street, with the bottle under his arm, he began to think.

"If all is true about this bottle, I may have made a losing bargain," thinks he. "But, perhaps, the man was only fooling me."

The first thing he did was to count his money; the sum was exact, forty-nine American dollars and one Chili piece.

"That looks like the truth," said Keawe. "Now I will try another part."

The streets in that part of the city were as clean as a ship's decks, and though it was noon, there were no passengers. Keawe set the bottle in the gutter and walked away. Twice he looked back, and there was the milky, round-bellied bottle where he left it. A third time he looked back and turned a corner; but he had scarce done so when something knocked upon his elbow, and behold! it was the long neck sticking up, and as for the round belly, it was jammed into the pocket of his pilot-coat.

"And that looks like the truth, too," said Keawe.

The next thing he did was to buy a corkscrew in a shop, and go apart into a secret place in the fields. And there he tried to draw the cork; but as often as he put the screw in, out it came again, and the cork as whole as ever.

"This is some new sort of cork," said Keawe; and all at once he began to shake and sweat, for he was afraid of that bottle.

On his way back to the port side, he saw a shop where a man sold shells and clubs from the wild islands, old heathen deities, old coined money, pictures from China and Japan, and all manner of things that sailors bring in their sea-chests. And here he had an idea. So he went in and offered the bottle for one hundred dollars. The man of the shop laughed at him at the first, and offered him five dollars, as indeed it was a curious bottle; such glass was never blown in any human glass-work, so prettily the colors shone under the milky-white, and so strangely the shadow hovered in the midst; so, after he had disputed awhile, after the manner of his kind, the shopman gave Keawe sixty silver dollars for the thing, and set it on a shelf in the midst of his window.

"Now," said Keawe, "I have sold that for sixty which I bought for fifty, or, to say the truth, a little less, because one of my dollars was from Chili. Now I shall know the truth upon another point."

So he went back on board his ship, and when he opened his chest there was the bottle, and it had come more quickly than himself. Now, Keawe had a mate on board, whose name was Lopaka.

"What ails you!" said Lopaka, "that you stare in your chest?"

They were alone in the ship's forecastle, and Keawe bound him to secrecy and told all.

"This is a very strange affair," said Lopaka, "and I fear you will be in trouble about this bottle. But there is one point very clear—that you are sure of the trouble, and you had better have the profit in the bargain. Make up your mind what you want with it, give the order, and if it is done as you desire, I will buy the bottle myself, for I have an idea of my own to get a schooner and go trading through the islands."

"That is not my idea," said Keawe; "but to have a beautiful house and garden on the Kona coast, where I was born, the sun shining in at the door, flowers in the garden, glass in the windows, pictures on the walls, and toys and fine carpets on the tables, for all the world like the house I was in this day, only a story higher, and with balconies all about, like the king's palace; and to live there without care, and make merry with my friends and relatives."

"Well," said Lopaka, "let us carry it back with us to

Hawaii, and if all comes true, as you suppose, I will buy the bottle, as I said, and ask a schooner."

Upon that they were agreed, and it was not long before the ship returned to Honolulu, carrying Keawe, and Lopaka, and the bottle. They were scarce come ashore, when they met a friend upon the beach, who began at once to condole with Keawe.

"I do not know what I am to be condoled about," said Keawe.

"Is it possible you have not heard?" said the friend, "Your uncle, that good old man, is dead, and your cousin, that beautiful boy, was drowned at sea."

Keawe was filled with sorrow, and beginning to weep and to lament, he forgot about the bottle. But Lopaka was thinking to himself, and presently, when Keawe's grief was a little abated, "I have been thinking," said Lopaka, "had not your uncle lands in Hawaii, in the district of Kau?"

"No," said Keawe, "not in Kau; they are on the mountain-side, a little besouth Hookena."

"These lands will now be yours?" asked Lopaka.

"And so they will," said Keawe, and began again to lament for his relatives.

"No," said Lopaka, "do not lament at present. I have a thought in my mind. How if this should be the doing of the bottle? For here is the place ready for your house."

"If this be so," cried Keawe, "it is a very ill way to serve me by killing my relatives. But it may be, indeed; for it was in just such a station that I saw the house with my mind's eye.

"The house, however, is not yet built," said Lopaka.

"No; nor like to be," says Keawe, "for though my uncle has some coffee, and ava, and bananas, it will not be more than will keep me in comfort; and the rest of that land is the black lava."

"Let us go to the lawyer," said Lopaka; "I have still this idea in my mind."

Now, when they came to the lawyer's it appeared Keawe's uncle had grown monstrous rich in the last days, and there was a fund of money.

"And here is the money for the house," cried Lopaka.

"If you are thinking of a new house," said the lawyer, "here is the card of a new architect, of whom they tell me great things."

"Better and better!" cried Lopaka. "Here is all made plain for us. Let us continue to obey orders."

So they went to the architect, and he had drawings of houses on his table.

"You want something out of the way," said the architect. "How do you like this?" and he handed a drawing to Keawe.

Now, when Keawe set eyes on the drawing he cried out aloud, for it was the picture of his thought exactly drawn.

"I am in for this house," thought he. "Little as I like the way it comes to me, I am in for it now, and I may as well take the good along with the evil."

So he told the architect all that he wished, and how he would have that house furnished, and about the pictures on the walls and the knickknacks on the fables; and then he asked the man plainly for how much he would undertake the whole affair.

The architect put many questions, and took his pen and made a computation; and when he had done he named the very sum that Keawe had inherited.

Lopaka and Keawe looked at each other and nodded.

"It is quite clear," thought Keawe, "that I am to have this house, whether or not. It comes from the devil, and I fear I will get little good by that. And of one thing I am sure, I will make no more wishes as long as I have this bottle. But with the house I am saddled, and I may as well take the good along with the evil."

So he made his terms with the architect, and they signed a paper; and Keawe and Lopaka took ship again and sailed to Australia; for it was concluded between them they should not interfere at all, but leave the architect and the bottle.imp to build and to adorn that house at their own pleasure.

The voyage was a good voyage, only all the time Keawe was holding in his breath, for he had sworn he would utter no more wishes and take no more favors from the devil. The time was up when they got back; the architect told them that the house was ready, and Keawe and Lopaka took a passage in the "Hall" and went down Kona ways to view the house and see if all had been done fitly, according to the thought that was in Keawe's mind.

II

NOW, the house stood on the mountain-side, visible to ships. Above, the forest ran up into the clouds of rain; below, the black lava fell in cliffs, where the kings of old lay buried. A garden bloomed about that house with every hue of flowers; and there was an orchard of Papaia on the one hand, and an orchard of fruit-bread on the other; and right in front, toward the sea, a ship's mast had been rigged up, and bore a flag. As for the house, it was three stories high, with great chambers and broad balconies on each; the windows were of glass so excellent that it was as clear as water and as bright as day; all manner of furniture adorned the chambers; pictures hung upon the walls in golden frames—pictures of ships, and men fighting, and of the most beautiful women, and of singular places. Nowhere in the world are there pictures of so bright a color as those Keawe found hanging in his house. As for the knickknacks, they were extraordinary fine; chiming clocks and musical-boxes, little men with nodding heads, books filled with pictures, weapons from all quarters of the world, and the most elegant puzzles to entertain the leisure of a solitary man. And as no one would care to live in such chambers, only to walk through and view them, the balconies were made so broad that a whole town might have lived upon them in delight; and Keawe knew not which to prefer, whether the back porch, where you got the land breeze, and looked upon the orchards and the flowers, or the front balcony, where you could drink the wind of the sea, and look down the steep wall of the mountain, and see the "Hall" going by once a week or so, between Hookena and the Hills of Pele, or the schooners plying up the coast for wood, and ava, and bananas.

When they had viewed all, Keawe and Lopaka sat on the porch.

"Well," asked Lopaka, "is it all as you designed?"

"Words cannot utter it," said Keawe. "It is better than I dreamed, and I am sick with satisfaction."

"There is but one thing to consider," said Lopaka. "All this may be quite natural, and the bottle imp have nothing whatever to say to it. If I were to buy the bottle and get no schooner after all, I should have put my hand in the fire for nothing. I gave you my word, I know, but yet I think you would not grudge me one more proof."

"I have sworn I would take no more favors," said Keawe. "I have gone already deep enough."

"This is no favor I am thinking of," replied Lopaka. "It is only to see the imp himself. There is nothing to be gained by that, and so nothing to be ashamed of, and yet if I once saw him I should be ashamed of the whole matter. So indulge me so far, and let me see the imp, and after that there is the money in my hand, and I will buy it."

"There is only one thing that I am afraid of," said Keawe. "The imp may be very ugly to view, and if you once set eyes on him you might be very undesirous of the bottle."

"I am a man of my word," said Lopaka. "And here is the money betwixt us."

"Very well," replied Keawe; "I have a curiosity myself. So come, let us have one look at you, Mr. Imp."

Now, as soon as that was said, the imp looked out of the bottle and in again, swift as a lizard; and there sat Keawe and Lopaka, turned to stone. The night had quite come before either found a thought to say or voice to say it with, and then Lopaka pushed the money over and took the bottle.

"I am a man of my word," said he, "and had need to be so, or I would not touch this bottle with my foot. Well, I shall get my schooner and a dollar or two for my pocket; and then I will be rid of this devil as fast as I can. For, to tell the plain truth, the look of him has cast me down."

"Lopaka," said Keawe, "do not think any worse of me than you can help. I know it is night, and the roads bad, and the pass by the tombs an ill place to go by so late; but I declare, since I have seen the little face I can not eat, or sleep, or pray till it is gone from me. I will give you a lantern and a basket to put the bottle in, and any picture or fine thing in my house that takes your fancy, and be gone at once, and go sleep at Hookena with Nahinu."

"Keawe," said Lopaka, "many a man would take this ill; above all, when I am doing you a turn so friendly as to keep my word and to buy the bottle, and, for that matter, the night, and the dark, and the way by the tombs must be all tenfold more dangerous to a man with such a sin upon his conscience and such a bottle under his arm. But for my part, I am so extremely terrified myself, I have not the heart to blame you. Here I go, then, and I pray God you may be happy in your house, and I fortunate with my schooner, and both get to heaven in the end, in spite of the devil and his bottle."

So Lopaka went down the mountain, and Keawe stood in his front balcony and listened to the clink of the horse's shoes and watched the lantern go shining down the path and along the cliff of caves, where the old dead are buried; and all the time he trembled and clasped his hands and prayed for his friend, and gave glory to God that he himself was escaped out of that trouble.

But the next day came very brightly, and that new house of his was so delightful to behold that he forgot his terrors. One day followed another, and Keawe dwelt there in perpetual joy. He had his place on the back porch; it was there he ate, and lived, and read the stories in the Honolulu newspapers; but when any one came by they would go in and view the chambers and the pictures. And the fame of the house went far and wide. It was called Ka-Hale Nui—the Great House—in all Kona; and sometimes the Bright House, for Keawe kept a Chinaman, who was all day dusting and furbishing, and the glass, and the gilt, and the fine stuffs, and the pictures shone as bright as the morning. As for Keawe himself, he could not walk in the chambers without singing, his heart was so enlarged; and when ships sailed by upon the sea he would fly his colors on the mast.

Some time went by until one day Keawe went upon

a visit as far as Kailua, to certain of his friends. There he was well feasted, and left as soon as he could the next morning, and rode hard, for he was impatient to behold his beautiful house, and besides, the night then coming on was the night in which the dead of old days go abroad in the sides of Kona; and having already meddled with the devil, he was the more chary of meeting with the dead. A little beyond Honaunau, looking far ahead, he was aware of a woman bathing in the edge of the sea; and she seemed a well-grown girl; but he thought no more of it. Then he saw her white shift flutter as she put it on, and then her red holoku, and by the time he came abreast of her she was done with her toilet and had come up from the sea and stood by the track-side in her red holoku, and she was all fresh with the bath, and her eyes shone and were kind. Now Keawe no sooner beheld her than he drew rein.

"I thought I knew every one in this country," he said. "How comes it that I do not know you?"

"I am Kokua, daughter of Kiano," said the girl, "and I have just returned from Oahu. Who are you?"

"I will tell you who I am in a little," said Keawe, dismounting from his horse, "but not now, for I have a thought in my mind, and if you knew who I was, you might have heard of me, and you would not give me a true answer. But tell me, first of all, one thing. Are you married?"

At this Kokua laughed out loud.

"It is you who ask questions," she said. "Are you married yourself?"

"Indeed, Kokua, I am not," replied Keawe, "and never thought to be until this hour. But here is the plain truth: I have met you here at the road-side and saw your eyes, which are like the stars, and my heart went to you swift as a bird. And so now, if you want none of me, say so, and I will go on to my own place; but if you think me no worse than any other young man, say so, too, and I will turn aside to your father's for the night, and to-morrow I will talk with the good man."

Kokua said never a word, but she looked at the sea and laughed.

"Kokua," said Keawe, "if you say nothing, I will take that for the good answer; so let us be stepping to your father's door."

She went on ahead of him, still without speech; only sometimes she glanced back, and glanced away again; and she kept the strings of her hat in her mouth.

Now, when they had come to the door, Kiano came out in his veranda, and cried out, and welcomed Keawe by name. At that the girl looked over, for the fame of the great house had come to her ears, and to be sure it was a great temptation. All that evening they were very merry together; and the girl was as bold as brass under the eyes of her parents, and made a mark of Keawe, for she had a quick wit. The next day he had a word with Kiano, and found the girl alone.

"Kokua," said he, "you made a mark of me all evening; and it is still time to bid me go. I would not tell you who I was, because I have so fine a house, and I feared you would think too much of that house and too little of the man that loves you. Now you know all, and if you wish to have seen the last of me, say so at once."

"No," said Kokua. But this time she did not laugh, nor did Keawe ask for more.

This was the wooing of Keawe; things had gone quickly, but so an arrow goes, and the ball of a rifle swifter still, and yet both may strike the target. Things had gone fast, but they had gone far also, and the thought of Keawe rang in the maiden's head; she heard his voice in the breach of the surf upon the lava, and for this young man that she had seen but twice she would have left father, and mother, and her native islands. As for Keawe himself, his horse flew up the path of the mountain under the cliff of tombs, and the sound of the hoofs, and the sound of Keawe singing to himself for pleasure, echoed in the caverns of the dead. He came to the Bright House, and still he was singing. He sat and ate in the broad balcony, and the Chinaman wondered at his master, to hear how he sung between the mouthfuls. The sun went down into the sea, and the night came, and Keawe walked the balconies by lamp-light, high on the mountain, and the voice of his singing startled men on ships.

"Here am I now upon my high place," he said to himself. "Life may be no better; this is the mountain-top, and all shelves about me toward the worse. For the first time I will light up the chambers, and bathe in my fine bath, with the hot water and the cold, and sleep above in the bed of my bridal-chamber."

So the Chinaman had word, and he must rise from sleep and light the furnaces; and as he walked below beside the boilers, he heard his master singing and rejoicing above him in the lighted chambers. When the water began to be hot, the Chinaman cried to his master, and Keawe went into the bath-room, and the Chinaman heard him sing as he filled the marble basin, and heard him sing again, the singing broken, as he undressed, until, of a sudden, the song ceased. The Chinaman listened and listened; he called up the house to Keawe, to ask him if all were well, and Keawe answered him "Yes," and bade him go to bed, but there was no more singing in the Bright House, and all night long the Chinaman heard his master's feet go round and round the balconies without repose.

Now the truth of it was this: As Keawe undressed for his bath, he spied upon his flesh a patch like a patch of lichen on a rock, and it was then that he stopped singing. For he knew the likeness of that patch, and he knew that he had fallen in the Chinese evil.

Now, it is a sad thing for any man to fall into this sickness. And it would be a sad thing for any one to leave a house so beautiful and so commodious, and depart from all his friends to the north coast of Molokai, between the mighty cliff and the sea-breakers. But what was that to the case of the man Keawe? He who had met his love but yesterday, and won her but that morning, and now saw all his hopes break in a moment like a piece of glass.

Awhile he sat upon the edge of the bath; then sprung, with a cry, and ran outside, and to and fro, and to and fro along the balcony like one despairing.

"Very willingly could I leave Hawaii, the home of my fathers," Keawe was thinking. "Very lightly could I leave my house, the high-placed, the many-windowed, here upon the mountains. Very bravely could I go to Molokai, to Kalaupapa by the cliffs, to live with the smitten, and to sleep there far from my fathers. But what wrong have I done, what sin lies upon my soul, that I should have encountered Kokua coming cool from the sea water in the evening—Kokua, the soul-ensnarer, Kokua, the light of my life? Her may I never wed, her may I look upon no longer, her may I no more handle with my loving hand. And it is for this—it is for you, oh, Kokua, that I pour my lamentations!"

Thereupon he called to mind it was the next day the "Hall" went by on her return to Honolulu.

"There I must go first," he thought, "and seek Lopaka. For the best hope that I have now is to find that same bottle I was so pleased to be rid of."

Now, you are to observe what kind of a man Keawe was, for he might have dwelt there in the Bright House for years, and no one been the wiser of his sickness; but he recked nothing of that if he must lose Kokua. And again he might have wed Kokua even as he was; and so many would have done, because they have the souls of pigs. But Keawe loved the maid manfully, and he would do her no hurt and bring her in no danger.

A little beyond the midst of the night came in his mind the recollection of that bottle. He went round to the back porch and called to memory the day when the devil had looked forth, and at the thought ice ran in his veins.

"A dreadful thing is the bottle," thought Keawe, "and dreadful is the imp, and it is a dreadful thing to risk the flames of hell. But what other hope have I to cure my sickness or to wed Kokua? What!" he thought, "would I beard the devil once only to get me a house, and not face him again to win Kokua?"

III

NEVER a wink could he sleep, the food stuck in his throat; but he sent a letter to Kiano, and about the time when the steamer would be coming rode down beside the cliff of the tombs. It rained; his horse went heavily; he looked up at the black mouths of caves, and he envied the dead that slept there and were done with trouble, and called to mind how he had galloped by the day before, and was astonished. So he came down to Hookena, and there was all the country gathered for the steamer, as usual. In the shed before the store they sat, and jested, and passed the news; but there was no matter of speech in Keawe's bosom, and he sat in their midst and looked without on the rain falling on the houses and the surf beating among the rocks, and the sighs arose in his throat.

"Keawe, of the Bright House, is out of spirits," said one to another.

Indeed, and so he was, and little wonder.

Then the "Hall" came, and the whale-boat carried him on board. The after-part of the ship was full of Haoles—whites—who had been to visit the volcano, as their custom is, and the midst was crowded with Kanakas, and the forepart with wild bulls from Hilo, and horses from Kau; but Keawe sat apart from all, in his sorrow, and watched for the house of Kiano. There it sat, low upon the shore, in the black rocks, and shaded by the cocoa-palms, and there by the door was a red holoku, no greater than a fly, and going to and fro with a fly's business.

"Ah! queen of my heart," he cried, "I will venture my dear soul to win you!"

Soon after darkness fell, and the cabins were lighted up, and the Haoles sat and played at the cards and drank whiskey, as their custom is; but Keawe walked the deck all night, and all the next day; as they steamed under the lee of Maui or of Molokai he was still pacing to and fro, like a wild animal in a menagerie.

Toward evening they passed Diamond Head and came to the pier of Honolulu. Keawe stepped out among the crowd and began to ask for Lopaka. It seemed he had become the owner of a schooner, none better in the islands, and was gone upon an adventure as far as Pola-Pola or Kahiki; so there was no help to be looked for from Lopaka. Keawe called to mind a friend of his, a lawyer in the town (I must not tell his name), and inquired of him; they said he had grown suddenly rich and had a fine new house upon Waikiki shore; and this put a thought in Keawe's head, and he called a hack and drove to the lawyer's house.

The house was all brand-new, and the trees in the garden no greater than walking-sticks, and the lawyer (when he came) had the air of a man well pleased.

"What can I do to serve you?" said the lawyer.

"You are a friend of Lopaka's," replied Keawe, "and Lopaka purchased from me a certain piece of goods that I thought you might enable me to trace."

The lawyer's face became very dark.

"I do not profess to misunderstand you, Mr. Keawe," said he, "though this is an ugly business to be stirring in. You may be sure I know nothing, but yet I have a guess; and if you would apply in a certain quarter, I think you might have news."

And he named the name of a man, which again I had better not repeat. So it was for days; and Keawe went from one to another, finding everywhere new clothes and carriages, and fine new houses, and men everywhere in great contentment; although (to be sure) when he hinted at his business, their faces would cloud over.

"No doubt, I am upon the track," thought Keawe. "These new clothes and carriages are all the gifts of the little imp, and these glad faces are the faces of men who have taken their profit and got rid of the accursed thing in safety. When I see pale cheeks and hear sighing, I shall know that I am near the bottle."

So it befell at last that he was recommended to a Haole in Beritania Street. When he came to the door, about the hour of the evening meal, there were the usual marks of the new house, and the young garden, and the electric light shining in the windows; but when the owner came a shock of hope and fear ran through Keawe. For here was a young man, white as a corpse and black about the eyes, the hair shedding from his head, and such a look in his countenance as a man may have when he is waiting for the gallows.

"Here it is, to be sure," thought Keawe; and so with this man he noways veiled his errand. "I am come to buy the bottle," said he.

At the word the young Haole of Beritania Street reeled against the wall.

"The bottle!" he gasped. "To buy the bottle?"

Then he seemed to choke, and seizing Keawe by the arm, carried him into the room and poured out wine in two glasses.

"Here is my respects," said Keawe, who had been much about with Haoles in his time. "Yes," he added, "I am come to buy the bottle. What is the price by now?"

At that word the young man let his glass slip through his fingers, and looked upon Keawe like a ghost.

"The price?" says he. "The price? You do not know the price?"

"It is for that I am asking you," returned Keawe.

"But why are you so much concerned? Is there anything wrong about the price?"

"It has dropped a great deal in value since your time, Mr. Keawe," said the young man, stammering.

"Well, well, I shall have the less to pay for it," says Keawe. "How much did it cost you?"

The young man was as white as a sheet.

"Two cents," said he.

"What!" cried Keawe; "two cents? Why, then, you can only sell it for one. And he who buys it—"

The words died upon Keawe's tongue. He who bought it could never sell it again; the bottle and bottle imp must abide with him until he died, and when he died must carry him to the red end of hell.

The young man of Beritania Street fell upon his knees.

"For God's sake, buy it!" he cried. "You can have all my fortune in the bargain. I was mad when I bought it at that price. I had embezzled money at my store; I was lost, else I must have gone to jail."

"Poor creature!" said Keawe. "You would risk your soul upon so desperate an adventure, and to avoid the proper punishment of your own disgrace; and you think I could hesitate with love in front of me. Give me the bottle and the change, which I make sure you have all ready. Here is a five-cent piece."

It was as Keawe supposed; the young man had the change ready in a drawer; the bottle changed hands, and Keawe's fingers were no sooner clasped upon the stalk than he had breathed his wish to be a clean man.

And sure enough, when he got home to his room and stripped himself before a glass, his flesh was whole, like an infant's. And here was the strange thing; he had no sooner seen this miracle than his mind was changed within him, and he cared naught for the Chinese evil, and little enough for Kokua; and had but one thought, that here he was bound to the bottle imp for time and for eternity, and had no better hope but to be cinder forever in the flames of hell. Away ahead of him he saw them blaze in his mind's eye, and his soul shrunk, and darkness fell upon the light.

When Keawe came to himself a little, he was aware it was the night when the band played at the hotel. Thither he went, because he feared to be alone; and there, among happy faces, walked to and fro, and heard the tunes go up and down, and saw Berger beat the measure, and all the while he heard the flames crackle, and saw the red fire burning in the bottomless pit. Of a sudden, the band played "Hiko-ao-ao"; that was a song that he had sung with Kokua, and at the strain courage returned to him.

"It is done now," he thought, "and once more let me take the good along with the evil."

So it befell that he returned to Hawaii by the first steamer, and as soon as it could be managed he was wedded to Kokua, and carried her up the mountainside to the Bright House.

Now it was so with these two that when they were together Keawe's heart was stilled, but so soon as he was alone he fell into a brooding horror, and heard the flames crackle, and saw the red fire burn in the bottomless pit. The girl, indeed, had come to him wholly; her heart leaped in her side at sight of him, her hand clung to his, and she was so fashioned from the hair upon her head to the nails upon her toes that none could see her without joy. She was pleasant in her nature. She had the good word always. Full of song she was, and went to and fro in the Bright House, the brightest thing in its three stories, caroling like birds. And Keawe beheld and heard her with delight, and then must shrink upon one side, and weep and groan to think upon the price that he had paid for her; and then he must dry his eyes, and wash his face, and go and sit with her on the broad balconies, joining in her songs and (with a sick spirit) answering her smiles.

There came a day when her feet began to be heavy and her songs more rare; and now it was not Keawe only that would weep apart, but each would sunder from the other, and sit in opposite balconies, with the whole width of the Bright House betwixt. Keawe was so sunk in his despair he scarce observed the change, and was only glad he had more hours to sit alone and brood upon his destiny, and was not so frequently condemned to pull a smiling face on a sick heart. But one day, coming softly through the house, he heard the sound of a child sobbing, and there was Kokua rolling her face upon the balcony floor and weeping like the lost.

"You do well to keep in the house, Kokua," he said, "and yet I would give the head off my body that you (at least) might have been happy."

"Happy!" she cried. "Keawe, when you lived alone in your Bright House, you were the word of the island for a happy man; laughter and song were in your mouth, and your face was as bright as the sunrise. Then you wedded poor Kokua, and the good God knows what is amiss in her, but from that day you have not smiled. Oh!" she cried, "what ails me? I thought I was pretty, and I know I loved him. What ails me that I throw this cloud upon my husband?"

"Poor Kokua," said Keawe. He sat down by her side and sought to take her hand, but that she plucked away. "Poor Kokua," he said again. "My poor child, my pretty! And I had thought all this while to spare you! Well, you shall know all. Then at least you will pity poor Keawe; then you will understand how much he has loved you in the past, that he dared hell for your possession, and how much he loves you still (the poor, condemned one), that he can yet call up a smile when he beholds you."

With that he told her all, even from the beginning.

"You have done this for me?" she cried. "Ah, well, then what do I care?" and she clasped and wept upon him.

"Ah, child!" said Keawe, "and yet, when I consider the fire of hell, I care a good deal!"

"Never tell me," said she. "No man can be lost because he loved Kokua, and no other fault. I tell you, Keawe, I shall save you with these hands, or perish in your company. What! you loved me, and you gave your soul, and you think I will not die to save you in return?"

"Ah, my dear, you might die a hundred times, and what difference would that make?" he cried, "except to leave me lonely till the time comes of my damnation."

"You know nothing," said she; "I was educated in a school in Honolulu; I am no common girl, and I tell you I shall save my lover. What is this you say about a cent? But all the world is not America. In England they have a piece called a farthing, which is about half a cent. Ah, sorrow!" she cried, "that makes it scarcely better, for the buyer must be lost, and we shall find none so brave as my Keawe! But, then, there is France; they have a small coin there which they call a centime, and these go five to the cent or thereabout. We could not do better. Come, Keawe, let us go to the French Islands; let us go to Tahiti as fast as ships can bear us. There we have four centimes, three centimes, two centimes, one centime; four possible sales to come and go on, and two of us to push the bargain. Come, my Keawe, kiss me, and banish care. Kokua will defend you."

"Gift of God," he cried, "I can not think that God will punish me for desiring aught so good! Be it as you will, then; take me where you please; I put my life and my salvation in your hands."

Early the next day, Kokua was about her preparations. She took Keawe's chest, that he went with sailoring, and first she put the bottle in the corner, and then packed it with the richest of their clothes and the bravest of the knickknacks in the house.

"For," said she, "we must seem to be rich folk, or who will believe in the bottle?"

All the time of her preparation she was as gay as a bird; only when she looked upon Keawe, the tears would spring in her eyes, and she must run and kiss him. As for Keawe, a weight was off his soul; now that he had his secret shared, and some hope in front of him, he seemed like a new man, his feet went lightly on the earth, and his breath was good to him again. Yet was terror still at his elbow; and ever and again, as the wind blows out a taper, hope died in him, and he saw the flames toss and the red fire burn in hell.

It was given out in the country they were gone pleasuring to the States, which was thought a strange thing, and yet not so strange as the truth, if any could have guessed it. So they went to Honolulu in the "Hall," and thence in the "Umatilla" to San Francisco, with a crowd of Haoles, and at San Francisco took their passage by the mail brigantine, the "Tropic Bird," for Papecte, the chief place of the French in the South Islands. Thither they came, after a pleasant voyage, on a fair day of the tradewind, and saw the reef with the surf breaking, and Motuti with its palms, and the schooners riding withinside, and the white houses of the town low down along the shore among green trees, and overhead the mountains and the clouds of Tahiti, the Wise Island.

It was judged the most wise to hire a house, which they did accordingly, opposite the British Consul's; to make a great parade of money, and themselves conspicuous with carriages and horses. This was very easy to do so long as they had the bottle in their possession, for Kokua was more bold than Keawe, and whenever she had a mind, called on the imp for twenty or a hundred dollars. At this rate they soon grew to be remarked in the town; and the strangers from Hawaii, their riding and their driving, the fine holokus and the rich lace of Kokua, became the matter of much talk.

They got on well after the first with the Tahitian language, which is like to the Hawaiian, with a change of certain letters; and as soon as they had any freedom of speech, began to push the bottle. You are to consider it was no easy subject to introduce; it was not easy to persuade people you were in earnest when you offered to sell them for four centimes the spring of health and riches inexhaustible. It was necessary, besides, to explain the dangers of the bottle; and either people disbelieved the whole thing and laughed, or they thought the more of the darker part, became overcast with gravity, and drew away from Keawe and Kokua as from persons who had dealings with the devil. So far from gaining ground, these two began to find they were avoided in the town; the children ran away from them screaming, a thing intolerable to Kokua; Catholics crossed themselves as they went by, and all persons began with one accord to disengage themselves from their advances.

Depression fell upon their spirits. They would sit at night in their new house, after a day's weariness, and not exchange one word; or the silence would be broken by Kokua bursting suddenly into sobs. Sometimes they would pray together, sometimes they would have the bottle out upon the floor and sit all evening watching how the shadow hovered in the midst. At such times they would be afraid to go to rest; it was long ere slumber came to them, and if either dozed off, it would be to wake and find the other silently weeping in the dark; or perhaps to wake alone, the other having fled from the house and the neighborhood of that bottle, to pace under the bananas in the little garden, or to wander on the beach by moonlight.

One night it was so when Kokua awoke. Keawe was gone; she felt in the bed, and his place was cold. Then fear fell upon her, and she sat up in bed. A little moonshine filtered through the shutters; the room was bright, and she could spy the bottle on the floor. Outside it blew high, the great trees of the avenue cried out aloud, and the fallen leaves rattled in the veranda. In the midst of this Kokua was aware of another sound; whether of a beast or of a man, she could scarce tell; but it was as sad as death, and cut her to the soul. Softly she arose, set the door ajar, and looked forth into the moonlit yard. There, under the bananas, lay Keawe, his mouth in the dust, and as he lay he moaned.

It was Kokua's first thought to run forward and console him. Her second potently withheld her. Keawe had borne himself before his wife like a brave man; it became her little in the hour of weakness to intrude upon his shame. With the thought she drew back into the house.

"Heaven!" she thought, "how careless have I been —how weak! It is he, not I, that stands in this eternal peril; it was he, not I, that took the curse upon his soul. It is for my sake, and for the love of a creature of so little worth and such poor help that he now beholds so close to him the flames of hell, ay, and smells the smoke of it, lying without there in the wind and moonlight. Am I so dull of spirit that never till now I have surmised my duty? or have I seen it before and turned aside? But now, at least, I take up my soul in both the hands of my affection; now I say farewell to the white steps of heaven and the waiting faces of my friends. A love for a love, and let mine be equaled with Keawe's! A soul for a soul, and let it be mine to perish!"

IV

THIS was a deft woman with her hands, and she was soon appareled. She took in her hands the change; the precious centimes they kept ever at their side, for this coin is little used, and they had made provision at a government office. When she was forth in the avenue, clouds came on the wind, and the moon was blackened. The town slept, and she knew not whither to turn till she heard some one coughing in the shadow of the trees.

"Old man," said Kokua, "what do you here abroad in the cold night?"

The old man could scarce express himself for coughing, but she made out that he was old and poor, and a stranger in the island.

"Will you do me a service?" said Kokua. "As one stranger to another, and as an old man to a young woman, will you help a daughter of Hawaii?"

"Ah!" said the old man, "so you are the witch from the eight islands? And even my old soul you seek to entangle. But I have heard of you, and defy your wickedness!"

"Sit down here," said Kokua, "and let me tell you a tale."

And she told him the story of Keawe from the beginning to the end.

"And now," said she, "I am his wife, whom he bought with his soul's welfare. And what should I do? If I went to him myself and offered to buy it, he will refuse. But if you go, he will sell it eagerly. I will await you here; you will buy it for four centimes, and I will buy it again for three. And the Lord strengthen a poor girl!"

"If you meant falsely," said the old man, "I think God would strike you dead."

"He would!" cried Kokua. "Be sure He would. I could not be so treacherous. God would not suffer it."

"Give me the four centimes and await me here," said the old man.

Now, when Kokua stood alone in the street, her spirit died. The wind roared in the trees, and it seemed to her the rushing of the flames of hell; the shadows tossed in the light of the street-lamps, and they seemed to her the snatching hands of evil ones. If she had had the strength, she must have run away, and if she had had the breath, she must have screamed aloud; but in truth she could do neither, and stood and trembled in the avenue like an affrighted child.

Then she saw the old man returning, and he had the bottle in his hand.

"I have done your bidding," said he, "I left your husband weeping like a child; to-night he will sleep easy."

And he held the bottle forth.

"Before you give it me," Kokua panted, "take the good with the evil—ask to be delivered from your cough."

"I am an old man," replied the other, "and too near the gate of the grave to take a favor from the devil. But what is this? Why do you not take the bottle? Do you hesitate?"

"Not hesitate!" cried Kokua. "I am only weak. Give me a moment. It is my hand resists; my flesh shrinks back from the accursed thing. One moment only!"

The old man looked upon Kokua kindly.

"Poor child!" said he, "you fear; your soul misgives you. Well, let me keep it. I am old, and can never more be happy in this world; and as for the next—"

"Give it me!" gasped Kokua. "There is your money. Do you think I am so base as that? Give me the bottle."

"God bless you, child," said the old man.

Kokua concealed the bottle under her holoku, said farewell to the old man, and walked off along the avenue, she cared not whither, for all roads were now the same to her, and led equally to hell. Sometimes she walked, and sometimes ran; sometimes she screamed out loud in the night, and sometimes lay by the way-side in the dust and wept. All that she had heard of hell came back to her; she saw the flames blaze, and she smelled the smoke, and her flesh withered on the coals.

Near day she came to her mind again, and returned to the house. It was even as the old man said, Keawe slumbered like a child. Kokua stood and gazed upon his face.

"Now, my husband," said she, "it is your turn to sleep. When you wake it will be your turn to sing and laugh. But for poor Kokua, alas! that meant no evil—for poor Kokua no more sleep, no more singing, no more delight, whether in earth or heaven."

With that she lay down in the bed by his side, and her misery was so extreme that she fell in a deep slumber instantly.

Late in the morning her husband woke her and gave her the good news. It seemed he was silly with delight, for he paid no heed to her distress, ill though she dissembled it. The words stuck in her mouth, it mattered not; Keawe did the speaking. She ate not a bite, but who was to observe it? For Keawe cleared the dish. Kokua saw and heard him, like some strange thing in a dream; there were times when she forgot or doubted, and put her hands to her brow; to know herself doomed and hear her husband babble, seemed so monstrous.

All the while Keawe was eating, and talking, and planning the time of their return, and thanking her for saving him, and fondling her, and calling her the true helper after all. He laughed at the old man that was fool enough to buy that bottle.

"A worthy old man, he seemed," Keawe said. "But no one can judge by appearances. For why did the old reprobate require the bottle?"

"My husband," said Kokua, humbly, "his purpose may have been good."

Keawe laughed like an angry man.

"Fiddle-de-dee!" cried Keawe. "An old rogue, I tell you. And an old ass, to boot. For the bottle was hard enough to sell at four centimes; at three it will be quite impossible. The margin is not broad enough; the thing begins to smell of scorching— b-r-r-r!" said he, and shuddered. "It is true, I bought it myself for a cent, when I knew not there were smaller coins. I was a fool for my pains; there will never be found another; and whoever has that bottle now will carry it to the pit."

"Oh, my husband!" said Kokua, "is it not a terrible thing to save ourselves by the eternal ruin of another? It seems to me I could not laugh; I would be humbled; I would be filled with melancholy; I would pray for the poor holder."

Then Keawe, because he felt the truth of what she said, grew the more angry. "Hoighty-toighty," cried he. "You may be filled with melancholy if you please. It is not the mind of a good wife. If you thought at all of me, you would sit shamed."

Thereupon he went out, and Kokua was alone.

What chance had she to sell the bottle at three

centimes? None, she perceived. And if she had any, here was her husband hurrying her away to a country where was nothing lower than a cent. And here—on the morrow of her sacrifice—here was her husband leaving her and blaming her!

She would not even try to profit by what time she had, but sat in the house, and now had the bottle out and viewed it with unutterable fear, and now with loathing, hid it out of sight.

By and by Keawe came back and would have her take a drive.

"My husband, I am ill," she said. "I am out of heart. Excuse me, I can take no pleasure."

Then was Keawe more wroth than ever with her because he thought she was brooding over the case of the old man, and with himself because he thought she was right and was ashamed to be so happy.

"This is your truth," cried he, "and this your affection! Your husband is just saved from eternal ruin, which he encountered for the love of you—and you can take no pleasure! Kokua, you have a disloyal heart."

He went forth again, furious, and wandered in the town all day. He met friends and drank with them; they hired a carriage and drove into the country, and there drank again. All the time Keawe was ill at ease because he was taking his pastime while his wife was sad, and because he knew in his heart that she was more right than he, and the knowledge made him drink the deeper.

Now, there was an old, brutal Haole drinking with

him—one that had been a boatswain of a whaler, a runaway, a digger in gold mines, a convict in prisons. He had a low mind and a foul mouth; he loved to drink and to see others drunken, and he pressed the glass upon Keawe. Soon there was no more money in the company.

"Here, you," says the boatswain, "you are rich, you have been always saying. You have a bottle or some foolishness."

"Yes," says Keawe, "I am rich. I will go back and get some money from my wife, who keeps it."

"That's a bad idea, mate," said the boatswain. "Never you trust a petticoat with dollars. They're all false as water; you keep an eye on her."

Now, this word stuck in Keawe's mind, for he was muddled with what he had been drinking.

"I should not wonder but what she was false, indeed," thought he. "Why else should she be so cast down at my release? But I will show her that I am not the man to be fooled. I will catch her in the act."

Accordingly, when they were back in town, Keawe bade the boatswain wait for him at the corner by the old calaboose, and went forward up the avenue alone to the door of his house. The night had come again; there was a light within, but never a sound; and Keawe crept about the corner, opened the back door softly, and looked in.

There was Kokua on the floor, the lamp at her side; before her was a milk-white bottle with a round belly and a long neck, and as she viewed it Kokua wrung her hands.

A long time Keawe stood and looked in the doorway. At first he was struck stupid, and then fear fell upon him that the bargain had been made amiss and the bottle had come back to him, as it came at San Francisco; and at that his knees were loosened, and the fumes of the wine departed from his head like mists off a river in the morning. And then he had another thought, and it was a strange one, that made his cheeks burn.

"I must make sure of this," thought he.

So he closed the door and went softly round the corner again, and then came noisily in as though he were but now returned.

And lo! by the time he opened the front door no bottle was to be seen, and Kokua sat in a chair and started up like one wakened out of sleep.

"I have been drinking all day and making merry," said Keawe. "I have been with good companions, and now I only come back for money and return to drink and carouse with them again."

Both his face and voice were stern as judgment, but Kokua was too troubled to observe.

"You do well to use your own, my husband," said she, and her words trembled.

"Oh, I do well in all things," said Keawe, and he went straight for the chest and took out money. But he looked, besides, in a corner where they kept the bottle, and there was no bottle there.

At that the chest heaved upon the floor like a sea-billow, and the house spun about him like a wreath of smoke; for he saw that he was lost now, and there was no escape.

"It is what I feared," he thought. "It is she who has bought it."

And then he came to himself a little and rose up, but the sweat streamed on his face as thick as the rain and as cold as the well water.

"Kokua," said he, "I said to you to-day what ill became me. Now I return to house with my jolly companions," and at that he laughed a little quietly, "I will take more pleasure in the cup if you forgive me."

She clasped his knees in a moment, she kissed his knees with flowing tears.

"Oh!" she cried, "I ask but a kind word!"

"Let us never think hardly of the other," said Keawe, and was gone out of the house.

Now, the money Keawe had taken was only some of that store of centime pieces they had laid in at their arrival. It was very sure he had no mind to be drinking. His wife had given her soul for him, now he must give his for hers; no other thought was in the world with him.

At the corner of the old calaboose there was the old boatswain waiting.

"My wife has the bottle," said Keawe, "and unless you help me to recover it there can be no more money and no more liquor to-night."

"You do not mean to say you are serious about that bottle?" cried the boatswain.

"There is the lamp," said Keawe. "Do I look as if I was jesting?"

"That is so," said the boatswain. "You look as serious as a ghost."

"Well, then," said Keawe, "here are three centimes; you must go to my wife in the house and offer her those for the bottle, which (if I am not much mistaken) she will give you instantly. Bring it to me here, and I will buy it back from you for two; for that is the law with this bottle, that is still must be sold for a less sum. But whatever you do, never breathe a word to her that you have come from me."

"Mate, I wonder, are you making a fool of me?" asked the boatswain.

"It will do you no harm if I am," returned Keawe.

"That is so, mate," said the boatswain.

"And if you doubt me," added Keawe, "you can try. As soon as you are clear of the house, wish to have your pocket full of money, or a bottle of the best rum, or what you please, and you will see the virtue of the thing."

"Very well, Kanaka," says the boatswain, "I will try; but if you are having your fun out of me, I will take my fun out of you with a belaying-pin."

So the whaleman went off up the avenue, and Keawe stood and waited. It was near the same spot where Kokua had waited the night before, but Keawe was more resolved, and never faltered in his purpose; only his soul was bitter with despair.

It seemed a long time he had to wait before he heard a voice singing in the darkness of the avenue. He knew the voice to be the boatswain's, but it was strange how drunken it appeared upon a sudden.

Next the man himself came stumbling into the light of the lamp. He had the devil's bottle buttoned in his coat; another bottle was in his hand, and even as he came in view he raised it to his mouth and drank.

"You have it," said Keawe. "I see that."

"Hands off!" cried the boatswain, jumping back. "Take a step near me, and I'll smash your mouth. You thought you could make a cat's-paw of me, did you?"

"What do you mean?" cried Keawe.

"Mean?" cried the boatswain. "This is a pretty good bottle, this is, that's what I mean. How I got it for three centimes I can't make out; but I'm sure you shan't have it for two."

"You mean you won't sell?" gasped Keawe.

"No, sir!" cried the boatswain. "But I'll give you a drink of the rum, if you like."

"I tell you," said Keawe, "the man who has that bottle goes to hell."

"I reckon I'm going, any way," returned the sailor, "and this bottle's the best thing to go with I've struck yet.

"No, sir," he cried again, "this is my bottle now, and you can go and fish for another."

"Can this be true?" Keawe cried. "For your own sake, I beseech you, sell it me!"

"I don't value any of your talk," said the boatswain. "You thought I was a flat; now you see I am not, and there's an end. If you won't have a swallow of rum, I'll have one myself. Here's your health, and good-night to you!"

So off he went down the avenue, toward town, and there goes the bottle out of the story.

But Keawe ran to Kokua light as the wind; and great was their joy that night, and great, since then, has been the peace of all their days in the Bright House.

NOTES

NOTES

THE SONG OF RAHÉRO

Introduction.—This tale, of which I have not consciously changed a single feature, I received from tradition. It is highly popular through all the country of the eight Tevas, the clan to which Rahéro belonged; and particularly in Taiárapu, the windward peninsula of Tahiti, where he lived. I have heard from end to end two versions; and as many as five different persons have helped me with details. There seems no reason why the tale should not be true.

Note 1, page 138. *"The aito,"* *quasi* champion, or brave. One skilled in the use of some weapon, who wandered the country challenging distinguished rivals and taking part in local quarrels. It was in the natural course of his advancement to be at last employed by a chief, or king; and it would then be a part of his duties to purvey the victim for sacrifice. One of the doomed families was indicated; the aito took his weapon and went forth alone; a little behind him bearers followed with the sacrificial basket. Sometimes the victim showed fight, sometimes prevailed; more often, without doubt, he fell. But whatever body was found, the bearers indifferently took up.

Note 2, page 140. *"Pai," "Honoura,"* and *"Ahupu."* Legendary persons of Tahiti, all natives of Taiárapu. Of the first two, I have collected singular although imperfect legends, which I hope soon to lay before the public in another place. Of Ahupu, except in snatches of song, little memory appears to linger. She dwelt at least about Tepari,—"the sea-cliffs,"— the eastern fastness of the isle; walked by paths known only to herself upon the mountains; was courted by dangerous suitors who came swimming from adjacent islands, and defended and rescued (as I gather) by the loyalty of native fish. My anxiety to learn more of "Ahupu Vehine" became (during my stay in Taiárapu) a cause of some diversion to that mirthful people, the inhabitants.

Note 3, page 142. *"Covered an oven."* The cooking fire is made in a hole in the ground, and is then buried.

Note 4, page 142. *"Flies."* This is perhaps an anachronism. Even speaking of to-day in Tahiti, the phrase would have to be understood as referring mainly to mosquitoes, and these only in watered valleys with close woods, such as I suppose to form the surroundings of Rahéro's homestead. Quarter of a mile away, where the air moves freely, you shall look in vain for one.

Note 5, page 144. *"Hook"* of mother-of-pearl. Bright-hook fishing, and that with the spear, appear to be the favourite native methods.

Note 6, page 145. *"Leaves,"* the plates of Tahiti.

Note 7, page 146. *"Yottowas,"* so spelt for convenience of pronunciation, *quasi* Tacksmen in the Scottish Highlands. The organisation of eight subdistricts and eight yottowas to a division, which was in use (until yesterday) among the Tevas, I have attributed without authority to the next clan.

Note 8, page 147. *"Ómare,"* pronounced as a dactyl. A loaded quarter-staff, one of the two favourite weapons of the Tahitian brave; the javelin, or casting spear, was the other.

Note 9, page 150. *"The ribbon of light."* Still to be seen (and heard) spinning from one marae to another on Tahiti; or so I have it upon evidence that would rejoice the Psychical Society.

Note 10, page 151. *"Námunu-úra."* The complete name is Namunu-ura te aropa. Why it should be pronounced Námunu, dactyllically, I cannot see, but so I have always heard it. This was the clan immediately beyond the Tevas on the south coast of the island. At the date of the tale the clan organisation must have been very weak. There is no particular mention of Támatéa's mother going to Papara, to the head chief of her own clan, which would appear her natural recourse. On the other hand, she seems to have visited various lesser chiefs among the Tevas, and these to have excused themselves solely on the danger of the enterprise. The broad distinction here drawn between Nateva and Námunu-úra is therefore not impossibly anachronistic.

Note 11, page 151. *"Hiopa the king."* Hiopa was really the name of the king (chief) of Vaiau; but I could never learn that of the king of Paea—pronounce to rhyme with the Indian *ayah*—and I gave the name where it was most needed. This note must appear otiose indeed to readers who have never heard of either of these two gentlemen; and perhaps there is only one person in the world capable at once of reading my verses and spying the inaccuracy. For him, for Mr. Tati Salmon, hereditary high chief of the Tevas, the note is solely written: a small attention from a clansman to his chief.

Note 12, page 152. *"Let the pigs be tapu."* It is impossible to explain *tapu* in a note; we have it as an English word, taboo. Suffice it, that a thing which was *tapu* must not be touched, nor a place that was *tapu* visited.

Note 13, page 159. *"Fish, the food of desire."* There is a special word in the Tahitian language to signify *hungering after fish*. I may remark that here is one of my chief difficulties about the whole story. How did king, commons, women, and all come to eat together at this feast? But it troubled none of my numerous authorities; so there must certainly be some natural explanation.

Note 14, page 164. *"The mustering word of the clan."*

> *Teva te ua,*
> *Teva te matai!*
>
> Teva the wind,
> Teva the rain!

Notes 15, and 16, page 171. *"The star of the dead."* Venus as a morning star. I have collected much curious evidence as to this belief. The dead retain their taste for a fish diet, enter into copartnery with living fishers, and haunt the reef and the lagoon. The conclusion attributed to the nameless lady of the legend would be reached to-day, under the like circumstances, by ninety per cent of Polynesians: and here I probably understate by one-tenth.

THE FEAST OF FAMINE

In this ballad, I have strung together some of the more striking particularities of the Marquesas. It rests upon no authority; it is in no sense, like "Rahéro," a native story; but a patchwork of details of manners and the impressions of a traveller. It may seem strange, when the scene is laid upon these profligate islands, to make the story hinge on love. But love is not less known in the Marquesas than elsewhere; nor is there any cause of suicide more common in the islands.

Note 1, page 175. *"Pit of Popoi."* Where the breadfruit was stored for preservation.

Note 2, page 175. *"Ruby-red."* The priest's eyes were probably red from the abuse of kava. His beard (*ib.*) is said to be worth an estate; for the beards of old men are the favourite head adornment of the Marquesans, as the hair of women formed their most costly girdle. The former, among this generally beardless and short-lived people, fetch to-day considerable sums.

Note 3, page 176. *"Tikis."* The tiki is an ugly image hewn out of wood or stone.

Note 4, page 180. *"The one-stringed harp."* Usually employed for serenades.

Note 5, page 181. *"The sacred cabin of palm."* Which, however, no woman could approach. I do not know where women were tattooed; probably in the common house, or in the bush, for a woman was a creature of small account. I must guard the reader against supposing Taheia was at all disfigured; the art of the Marquesan tattooer is extreme; and she would appear to be clothed in a web of lace, inimitably delicate, exquisite in pattern, and of a bluish hue that at once contrasts and harmonises with the warm pigment of the native skin. It would be hard to find a woman more becomingly adorned than "a well-tattooed" Marquesan.

Note 6, page 184. *"The horror of night."* The Polynesian fear of ghosts and of the dark has been already referred to. Their life is beleaguered by the dead.

Note 7, page 185. *"The quiet passage of souls."* So, I am told, the natives explain the sound of a little wind passing overhead unfelt.

Note 8, page 188. *"The first of the victims fell."* Without doubt, this whole scene is untrue to fact. The victims were disposed of privately and some time before. And indeed I am far from claiming the credit of any high degree of accuracy for this ballad. Even in a time of famine, it is probable that Marquesan life went far more gaily than is here represented. But the melancholy of to-day lies on the writer's mind.

TICONDEROGA

Introduction.—I first heard this legend of my own country from that friend of men of letters, Mr. Alfred Nutt, "there in roaring London's central stream," and since the ballad first saw the light of day in *Scribner's Magazine,* Mr. Nutt and Lord Archibald Campbell have been in public controversy on the facts. Two clans, the Camerons and the Campbells, lay claim to this bracing story; and they do well: the man who preferred his plighted troth to the commands and menaces of the dead is an ancestor worth disputing. But the Campbells must rest content: they have the broad lands and the broad page of history; this appanage must be denied them; for between the name of *Cameron* and that of *Campbell,* the muse will never hesitate.

Note 1, page 203. Mr. Nutt reminds me it was "by my sword and Ben Cruachan" the Cameron swore.

Note 2, page 207. *"A periwig'd lord of London."* The first Pitt.

Note 3, page 208. *"Cathay."* There must be some omission in General Stewart's charming *History of the Highland Regiments,* a book that might well be republished and continued; or it scarce appears how our friend could have got to China.

HEATHER ALE

Among the curiosities of human nature, this legend claims a high place. It is needless to remind the reader that the Picts were never exterminated, and form to this day a large proportion of the folk of Scotland: occupying the eastern and the central parts, from the Firth of Forth, or perhaps the Lammermoors, upon the south, to the Ord of Caithness on the north. That the blundering guess of a dull chronicler should have inspired men with imaginary loathing for their own ancestors is already strange: that it should have begotten this wild legend seems incredible. Is it impossible the chronicler's error was merely nominal? that what he told, and what the people proved themselves so ready to receive, about the Picts, was true or partly true of some anterior and perhaps Lappish savages, small of stature, black of hue, dwelling underground —possibly also the distillers of some forgotten spirit? See Mr. Campbell's *Tales of the West Highlands.*